THE ST@Y HOME CHEF

SLOW COOKER COOKBOOK

THE STAY @ HOME CHEF

SLOW COOKER COOKBOOK

120 RESTAURANT-QUALITY RECIPES YOU CAN EASILY MAKE AT HOME

RACHEL FARNSWORTH

Reprinted and updated from *Idiot's Guides®: Slow Cooker Cooking*

Publisher Mike Sanders
Repackage Editor Brook Farling
Repackage Designer Lindsay Dobbs
Photographer Kelley Jordan Schuyler
Food Stylist Chung Lin Chow
Chef Tracey Couillard
Proofreader Lisa Himes
Indexer Louisa Emmons

First American Edition, 2021
Published in the United States by DK Publishing
6081 E. 82nd Street, Indianapolis, IN 46250

21 22 23 24 10 9 8 7 6 5 4 3
003-322403-SEP2021

ISBN: 978-0-7440-2918-5
Library of Congress Catalog Number: 2021931001

Note: This publication contains the opinions and ideas of its author(s). It is intended to provide helpful and informative material on the subject matter covered. It is sold with the understanding that the author(s) and publisher are not engaged in rendering professional services in the book. If the reader requires personal assistance or advice, a competent professional should be consulted. The author(s) and publisher specifically disclaim any responsibility for any liability, loss, or risk, personal or otherwise, which is incurred as a consequence, directly or indirectly, of the use and application of any of the contents of this book.

DK books are available at special discounts when purchased in bulk for sales promotions, premiums, fund-raising, or educational use. For details, contact: SpecialSales@dk.com

Printed and bound in Mexico

For the curious

www.dk.com

Introduction

Welcome to the wonderful world of slow cooking! Whether you are new to the slow cooker, or are just looking for more ways to utilize it, this book has been designed to meet the needs of home cooks of all skill levels. The recipes in this book are made from scratch wherever possible and plausible. Preparation times have been kept to an absolute minimum to maximize the convenience of the slow cooker, but without sacrificing quality. My culinary endeavors have taken me many places, but I am, first and foremost, a home cook just like you. I know how life goes, and I know exactly why you want to incorporate the slow cooker into your life. This handy appliance is a valuable tool in the kitchen and, when used properly, can produce stunning dishes. Not every recipe is best suited for slow cooking, but it's certainly a great cooking method that can be used for a wide array of dishes. It will add convenience—and delicious flavor—to your menu.

The 120 recipes in this book are designed to showcase the slow cooker's wide range of capabilities, while still presenting classic family-friendly dishes your family will enjoy. I've included lots of notes and tips throughout the book as well as pointers on ingredients and cooking methods—both for slow cooker cooking and cooking in general. Even if you're an experienced slow cooker cook, it's my hope that you'll find new ideas and inspiration in the pages that follow.

Acknowledgments

This book would not have been possible without my huge support team who has helped me every step of the way. First and foremost, credit must be given to my husband, Stephen, who supports me in my crazy dreams, late work nights, and culinary successes—and failures. A special thanks to my mother, who coached me with her artistic abilities. I love you, Mom! My children put up with a lot for this book, and I appreciate their patience, independence, and unfeigned love for their mother's cooking. You two are my little sous chefs, and although I could have worked faster and more efficiently without you, there just wouldn't have been as much love in the food. Thank you to the team of taste testers and friends who devoured the food shown in this book. You know who you are. I cannot possibly forget the people who make me look good—my personal team at The Stay at Home Chef, Dallan Anderson, Mike Downie, and Stephanie Patterson, alongside my team at Alpha Books, Brook Farling, Christy Wagner, and William Thomas.

About the Author

Rachel Farnsworth is the recipe developer and food writer behind the popular website known as The Stay at Home Chef (www.thestayathomechef.com). Her recipes are enjoyed by millions of people around the world each month. She believes that anyone can cook restaurant-quality meals at home and become the chef of their own kitchen. Rachel lives in the Salt Lake City area with her husband and two children.

Contents

CHAPTER 1

Slow Cooker Fundamentals

Welcome to the world of slow cooking—where the magic of low heat and slow cook times come together to yield flavorful recipes. You can simply prep the ingredients, place them in the slow cooker, and let this handy appliance do the rest of the work.

This book is full of recipes, tips, and tricks that will help you make the most of your slow cooker. In this chapter, you'll learn how slow cookers work, pick up some food safety essentials, and explore how to troubleshoot some common problems you may encounter along the way.

A

B

C

Getting to Know Your Slow Cooker

Slow cooking is one of the easiest and most convenient ways to cook. And while slow cookers have been around for a long time, they've come a long way since the early days of the Crock-Pot®. Before you get started, it's good to familiarize yourself with this handy appliance and how it works.

Components

The humble slow cooker consists of just a few basic components: a lid (A), a stoneware insert (B), and a heating base unit (C). The stoneware insert is where you place the food, and it fits inside the heating base unit, which is what slowly heats up the insert and cooks the food. The lid is most commonly made of glass, which allows you to see the food as it cooks, so you don't have to remove it and let out all that precious heat and steam. Some slow cookers also include latches to secure the lid for easy transportation of the cooked food. In addition to traditional slow cookers, many of today's multicooker appliances also feature slow cooker settings and may have slightly different components, but they all work pretty much the same, and the recipes in this book will work for all types of slow cookers.

Shapes and Sizes

Today's slow cookers come in multiple shapes and sizes, with the most common shapes being oval and round. Oval slow cookers are popular because they can hold odd-shaped roasts with ease, while round slow cookers tend to be deeper and allow ingredients to be stacked. Slow cooker sizes are measured in quarts. The smallest size available is a 1-quart (1-liter), while the largest slow cookers can hold up to 12 quarts (11.5 liters). Unless otherwise noted, the recipes in this book are designed for the most common size range of 6 to 8 quarts (5.5 to 7.5 liters).

Settings

The controls on today's slow cookers range from very basic to sophisticated. Most basic slow cookers will have three cook settings: low, high, and warm, but more sophisticated models have digital timers, are programmable, and might even feature wireless capabilities that allow you to use your smartphone to control the appliance. Many of today's multicooker appliances also feature a slow cooker setting.

The settings on a slow cooker refer to the wattage the heating element uses as it's cooking, and not necessarily the actual temperature the slow cooker reaches. There is no standard temperature for slow cookers, so there can be variation among models. Because of this, the cooking times can vary, depending on which model you use.

The ideal temperature range for slow cooking is 190°F to 210°F (90°C to 100°C). Most slow cookers have a maximum high temperature of 200°F (95°C), but some can reach 300°F (150°C). Most dishes should reach the ideal temperature range within several hours on the low setting, and in less than 1 hour on high. On most models, the high setting simply means the appliance reaches the temperature faster, but on some models it can mean the unit reaches a higher temperature. Check your owner's manual to learn how hot your slow cooker can get. The warm setting is designed to keep foods at a consistent food-safe temperature of at least 140°F (60°C). Food can be safely held on the warm setting for up to 4 hours. Most models will automatically switch to the warm setting after the programmed cook time is over, while some will automatically switch to the warm setting after 8 hours.

Slow Cooker Dos and Don'ts

Slow cookers offer so many advantages: They cook food evenly, and because they cook at lower temperatures for longer periods of time, they eliminate some of the more common issues like overcooking and burning that are associated with traditional cooking methods. But there are still some small things you can do to ensure your recipes always come out perfectly.

Do...

Use the low setting for most recipes
Unless a recipe specifically calls for using the high setting, you should always use the low setting to cook. Most foods will turn out best if cooked on the low setting. Some foods, and meats in particular, can taste watery and "boiled" when cooked on the high setting, and some softer vegetables can turn to mush if cooked on the high setting, particularly if they're cooked for longer periods of time.

Preheat the slow cooker
It isn't always necessary, but preheating can help kickstart the cooking process and get the ingredients up to temperature more quickly.

Place longer-cooking ingredients in the bottom of the slow cooker
Placing slower cooking ingredients like large cuts of meat in the bottom of the slow cooker means they have more direct access to the bottom heat source and cook more quickly.

Place faster-cooking ingredients in the top of the slow cooker
Faster-cooking ingredients, like vegetables, generally cook faster than meats, so you should layer them toward the top of the cooker, unless

otherwise noted in the recipe. Root vegetables like potatoes are the exception, as they will require longer cook times.

Keep the lid on
Unless the recipe indicates otherwise, always keep the lid on your slow cooker. Removing the lid allows heat to escape, and it can take up to 30 minutes for the slow cooker to get back up to the appropriate cooking temperature.

Brown large cuts of meat before adding them to the cooker
One of the few disadvantages of slow cooking is that you can't get that nice brown crust on larger cuts of meat. If you prefer that crust, simply brown the cuts on the stovetop before adding them to the slow cooker.

Trim excessively fatty cuts of meat
Another advantage of slow cooking is that it can break down tougher cuts of meat until they're fork-tender. This also means that most of the fat and connective tissue in the cut will be rendered into liquid, so recipes that use fatty cuts could end up with a lot of oil in the finished dish. Trimming some of the excess fat will help ensure the recipe doesn't end up too greasy.

Don't...

Place frozen ingredients in a slow cooker
With few exceptions, such as frozen meat-filled pastas that have already been cooked before being frozen, all meat should be thawed before being added to the slow cooker. Otherwise, the ingredients won't reach a safe temperature in time to prevent the growth of bacteria.

Underfill or overfill your slow cooker
A slow cooker should never be less than one third full and never more than three quarters full. Overfilling or underfilling can result in recipes being overcooked or undercooked, or being cooked unevenly.

Store cooked food in the insert
Unless otherwise noted, cooked food should always be cooled and then transferred to food-safe storage containers before being placed in the refrigerator or freezer. Sudden temperature changes can cause the stoneware insert to crack, which can be dangerous, so you should never place the insert in the refrigerator or freezer.

Use a slow cooker to reheat food
Any previously cooked food should be reheated on the stovetop or in a microwave oven.

Add too much liquid
Because the slow cooker is covered, almost no evaporation takes place during the slow cooking process, so less liquid is needed compared to other conventional cooking processes. Add only the amount of liquid that the recipe calls for, and if you find that your dishes still come out a bit soggy, try slightly reducing the amount of liquid the next time you make the recipe.

Use metal utensils or sharp knives in the insert
Metal can scratch and damage the surface of the insert, eventually making it more difficult to clean and potentially unusable. You should only use plastic, wood, or rubber utensils when stirring, cutting, or serving cooked foods.

Guess at the cooking temperature
Most foods, and meats, in particular, need to be cooked to specific temperatures to be safe. Always use a food thermometer to ensure your food is cooked properly.

Don't be afraid to experiment!
One of the bonuses of slow cooking is how versatile the slow cooking method is. Unless a recipe calls for a specific type of apple, onion, milk, or other ingredient, you can use whatever variety you prefer. As a general rule, most recipes in this book will specify which variety of ingredient to use, but if it doesn't, or you simply want to try something different, you can experiment to see what you like best. For instance, if you're making applesauce and prefer a more tart flavor, you might use Granny Smith apples. If you prefer a sweeter applesauce, however, Honeycrisp apples would be a better choice. If you prefer a sharper onion flavor, a recipe that calls for red onion might suit your tastes better by substituting a white onion. Making a recipe like bread pudding with whole milk instead of skim milk can add unique flavors and textures to the recipe. (The majority of the recipes in this book call for 2% milk, but you can substitute any other variety.) Don't be afraid to experiment to find just the right combination of ingredients that makes your mouth water.

Troubleshooting Tips

While slow cookers are incredibly easy to use, there are a few potential issues that can crop up. Here are some common problems that home cooks often encounter when slow cooking, along with some simple solutions.

What to do if your food is burning

If you find your food is burning in your slow cooker, it could mean your slow cooker is running hot. You can test the temperature of your slow cooker by performing this simple test:

1. Fill the stoneware insert two thirds full with water.
2. Cover the cooker and turn it on, using either the low or high settings.
3. Let the cooker run for 8 hours on low or 4 hours on high.
4. After the time has expired, quickly remove the lid and insert an instant-read thermometer in the water.

Whether you ran the test on the low or high settings, the water temperature should read between 190°F (90°C) and 210°F (100°C). Both settings reach the same temperature range in a slow cooker, the high setting just reaches the normal temperature range more quickly, which is why it requires shorter cooking times. If the temperature of the water is on the higher end of the normal range, you can try decreasing the cook times. If reducing the cook times doesn't solve the problem, or if you discover the water temperature is between 210°F (100°C) and 300°F (150°C), your unit may be broken and you may need to consider purchasing a new one.

What to do if one side of your slow cooker is burning your food

The side of the slow cooker's heating unit that's opposite the control unit on the front generally tends to run hotter and can burn food. To lessen this effect, you create a heat barrier by simply folding a 12-inch (30cm) piece of aluminum foil lengthwise in half three times and placing it against the wall of the insert on the hot side of the cooker. You can also use the same trick on any other area of the unit that tends to burn food. This method is particularly useful with breads and casseroles, which can burn easily. If you prefer not to use aluminum foil, you can simply rotate the insert halfway through the cooking time to ensure more even cooking.

What to do if your casseroles are coming out soggy

Slow cookers are perfect for cooking casseroles, but they sometimes can come out soggy, which is usually the result of using too much liquid in the recipe. If you encounter this problem, try decreasing the liquid the next time you make the recipe. In the meantime, cooking the recipe for an additional 30 to 60 minutes on high with the lid off will allow for quick evaporation and help minimize the sogginess.

How to remove those ugly spots on the stoneware insert

Normal wear and tear, and even hard water, are the most common causes of those annoying spots on your stoneware insert. You can remove some stubborn spots and stains by making a paste of baking soda and water, and scrubbing the paste onto the spots. Let the paste sit for 20 minutes and then rinse away the residue. You can also use a slow cooker liner to minimize the mess and make clean-up quick and easy. Liners are generally sold in the same area of grocery stores where you find aluminum foil, parchment paper, and plastic storage bags. If you can't remove all of the spots, don't fret; unless these areas affect how your food cooks, they're probably nothing to worry about and shouldn't affect the final results.

How to prevent rice and pasta from sticking to the insert

Rice and pasta can present some particularly challenging clean-up situations. To prevent rice or pasta from sticking to the sides of the insert, try using slow cooker liners or lining the entire insert with aluminum foil before you add the ingredients. You should be able to simply lift the insert or foil out of the cooker and clean-up should be simple.

How to prevent breads from burning

Because slow cooker breads can sometimes burn on the side where the stoneware gets the hottest, you can place a protective aluminum foil heat barrier in the area where the cooker gets the hottest. Another trick is to use a traditional bread pan, just so long as it fits in your cooker. If you do use a bread pan, note that the cook time will need to be a bit longer, but you'll avoid any burned edges or uncooked centers that can occur by cooking the bread directly in the insert.

What to do if the electricity goes out

If you're home while the slow cooker is cooking and the electricity goes out, all is not lost. First, make sure you keep the lid on to keep the heat in the unit. If the power resumes within 30 minutes, you can safely continue cooking your food. If the power does not resume within 30 minutes, you'll either need to find an alternate cooking method or you should discard the food. If you discover that the power went out while you were away and you don't know how long the electricity was off, it's best just to discard the food.

Other Helpful Slow Cooking Tips

Using a slow cooker is so incredibly simple, but there are some general things that are good to know as you begin to make the recipes in this book. Here are some tips that will make slow cooking even easier.

Using the Recipes in This Book

One of the wonderful things about slow cooking is how easy it is to get excellent results. Slow cookers are designed to cook slowly and gradually, compared with conventional cooking methods that use much higher cooking temperatures. This means that the need for exact cooking times is eliminated, and you can often cook within a range of time and still get excellent results. Because of this, most recipes in this book include a range of cooking times, and cooking your recipes for any time within that range, at the specified temperature setting, should still garner excellent results. If the cooking time for a recipe is more specific and does not include a range, you should stick to the specified time more closely, but you should still be able to pull the recipe from the cooker within a reasonable timeframe and still experience excellent results.

Preparing Recipes for Later Cooking

Although the nature of slow cooking means you can prepare your meal, fill the slow cooker, and let the appliance do the work for you, you should never fill it and then set it to turn on at a later time. Doing so means you'll be leaving the ingredients to sit out at room temperature, increasing the possibility of bacterial growth.

A better, safer alternative is to prepare the ingredients ahead of time, place them in a large bowl or storage container, and store them in the refrigerator until you're ready to cook. When you're ready to cook, preheat the slow cooker for 20-30 minutes, transfer the ingredients to the cooker, and then cook the recipe on the low setting. It's best not to store the prepared ingredients in the insert because placing a cold insert in the unit and exposing it to heat could damage it. If you do opt to store the ingredients in the insert, you should always select the low setting to avoid damaging the insert; the slow warming from the low setting will prevent the vessel from cracking. Likewise, you should never store your insert in the freezer or place a hot stoneware insert in the refrigerator or freezer. Both scenarios could damage the insert and cause it to crack or break, which could potentially be very dangerous, particularly if the insert is full of hot food.

Cooking Food Safely

The United States Department of Agriculture recommends that meats be cooked to the temperatures shown in the following table. If you're located outside of the U.S., you should check your country's guidelines for the temperature standards in your area.

Food	Minimum Internal Temperature
Poultry	165°F (75°C)
Casseroles	165°F (75°C)
Ground meats	160°F (70°C)
Eggs	160°F (70°C)
Beef, pork, veal, and lamb (steaks, chops, and roasts)	145°F (65°C)
Fish and shellfish	145°F (65°C)
Uncooked ham (fresh or smoked)	145°F (65°C)
Fully cooked ham	140°F (60°C)

Slow Cooker Cleaning and Care

A slow cooker's stoneware insert and glass lid usually are dishwasher safe, but you should check your owner's manual to see if your model is an exception. If they're not dishwasher safe, you can safely wash them by hand using a soft sponge, mild dish soap, and hot water.

If you notice a baked-on ring has formed in the stoneware insert, or if a recipe has left a particularly challenging clean-up situation, fill the insert with enough water to cover the ring or cooked-on food. Turn the slow cooker to the low setting and let it heat for 1 to 2 hours. After a few hours, you should be able to scrub the insert clean with a soft sponge and a little mild dish soap. You should never use abrasive cleaning compounds or pads on the insert, as these can damage the surface.

If the outside of the base unit becomes dirty, first unplug it and then try wiping it clean with a damp cloth. For particularly stubborn messes, try using oven cleaner, but be sure to do this in an area with plenty of ventilation, as many oven cleaners contain toxic chemicals. Also, be careful not to use too much water when cleaning the base unit; it contains the electrical components of the appliance and can become damaged and potentially a shock hazard if those parts get wet. Also, never submerge the base unit in water. Doing so can be very dangerous and also permanently damage the unit.

CHAPTER 2

Breakfasts

Slow cooker breakfasts are so convenient! The rush
of weekday morning routines doesn't always leave
much time for hot, nutritious breakfasts, but
the slow cooker changes that.

In this chapter, I share some fresh takes on breakfast
classics and give you everything you need to know
to enjoy the most important meal of the day.

Apple-Cinnamon Steel-Cut Oatmeal

Sweet apples and warm cinnamon combine for a flavorful overnight breakfast that utilizes the whole-grain goodness of steel-cut oats. Be prepared to wake up to a house filled with an amazing aroma!

YIELD	SERVING SIZE	PREP TIME	COOK TIME
5 CUPS	**¾ CUP**	**5 MINUTES**	**6 TO 8 HOURS**

1½ cups uncooked steel-cut oats

2½ cups apple juice

1½ cups reduced fat (2%) milk

1 large apple (any variety), peeled, cored, and diced

2 tbsp brown sugar (light or dark)

1 tsp ground cinnamon

¼ tsp salt

1 Grease a 2- or 3-quart (2- or 3-liter) slow cooker with shortening or oil, or spray with nonstick cooking spray.

2 In the slow cooker, combine the oats, apple juice, milk, apple, brown sugar, cinnamon, and salt.

3 Cover and cook on low for 6 to 8 hours. Store the leftovers in the refrigerator for up to 4 days.

VARIATION: Top with raisins, walnuts, pecans, or dried fruit.

TIP: Be sure to use steel-cut oats in this recipe as they will hold up best to the long cooking time. Regular oatmeal will break down and become mushy.

By the Way

This recipe is best made in a 2- or 3-quart (2- to 3-liter) slow cooker. Using a larger slow cooker could cause the oatmeal to burn. If you want to use a larger slow cooker, be sure to double or triple the recipe to avoid burning the oatmeal.

Brownie Batter Oatmeal

Who says you can't have dessert for breakfast? This oatmeal is full of chocolatey deliciousness, and the sweetness of the brown sugar counteracts the bitterness of the cocoa powder to produce a perfectly chocolate bite with every spoonful.

YIELD	SERVING SIZE	PREP TIME	COOK TIME
5 CUPS	**¾ CUP**	**5 MINUTES**	**6 TO 8 HOURS**

1½ cups uncooked steel-cut oats

4 cups reduced fat (2%) milk

½ cup unsweetened cocoa powder

½ cup brown sugar (light or dark), firmly packed

2 tsp pure vanilla extract

1 Grease a 2- or 3-quart (2- or 3-liter) slow cooker with shortening or oil, or spray with nonstick cooking spray.

2 In the slow cooker, combine the oats, milk, cocoa powder, brown sugar, and vanilla extract.

3 Cover and cook on low for 6 to 8 hours. Store in the refrigerator for up to 4 days.

VARIATION: For **German Chocolate Oatmeal,** use 2 cups unsweetened coconut milk instead of dairy milk.

TIP: If you don't have steel-cut oats, you can use rolled oats, but the oatmeal will be more porridge-like. Decrease the cooking time to 4 to 6 hours if you opt for rolled oats.

By the Way

Steel-cut oats are the best oats to use in slow cooker recipes. Their minimal processing requires a longer cooking time than old-fashioned, quick, or instant oats, which are all more processed.

Pumpkin Pie Oatmeal

Wake up to the nostalgic and comforting flavors of pumpkin pie with this delicious breakfast oatmeal. This recipe embraces the flavors of fall and provides a pleasantly sweet start on those crisp fall mornings.

YIELD	SERVING SIZE	PREP TIME	COOK TIME
5 CUPS	**¾ CUP**	**5 MINUTES**	**6 TO 8 HOURS**

1 cup uncooked steel-cut oats

4 cups reduced fat (2%) milk

¼ cup brown sugar (light or dark), firmly packed

1 tbsp pumpkin pie spice

1 tsp pure vanilla extract

¼ tsp salt

1 cup pumpkin purée

1 Grease a 2- or 3-quart (2- or 3-liter) slow cooker with shortening or oil, or spray with nonstick cooking spray.

2 In the slow cooker, combine the steel-cut oats, milk, brown sugar, pumpkin pie spice, vanilla extract, and salt.

3 Cover and cook on low for 6 to 8 hours. Stir in the pumpkin purée when ready to serve. (Adding the pumpkin purée at the end of the cooking process will help retain the rich pumpkin flavor.) Store in the refrigerator for up to 4 days.

TIP: To make this recipe vegan, substitute 3½ cups almond milk for the dairy milk. (The almond milk adds a nutty element that complements the flavors of the pumpkin pie.)

By the Way

Pumpkin pie spice is a mixture of cinnamon, nutmeg, ginger, and allspice. You can find it in the spice section of your grocery store.

Loaded Southwestern Hash Browns

In this recipe, traditional hash browns are loaded with fresh veggies and cheese. The pepper jack, jalapeño, bacon, and bell pepper all add a Southwestern flair and a little heat to this breakfast favorite.

YIELD	SERVING SIZE	PREP TIME	COOK TIME
6 CUPS	**1 CUP**	**30 MINUTES**	**6 TO 8 HOURS**

5 strips bacon

3 large russet potatoes, peeled

1 cup reduced fat (2%) milk

¾ cup shredded pepper jack cheese

¾ cup shredded cheddar cheese

1 large red bell pepper, seeded, ribs removed, and diced

5 large button or cremini mushrooms, sliced

2 tbsp sliced green onions

1 jalapeño, stemmed, seeded, and diced

½ tsp salt

¼ tsp freshly ground black pepper

1 Place a large skillet over medium heat. Cook the bacon for 10 minutes, then flip and cook for 7 to 10 minutes more or until crispy. Transfer the bacon to a paper towel–covered plate to drain. Set aside.

2 Using the largest grate on a box grater, shred the potatoes. Squeeze the potato shreds to remove any excess moisture and then place the potatoes in a large bowl.

3 To the bowl with the potatoes, add the milk, pepper jack cheese, cheddar cheese, red bell pepper, mushrooms, green onions, jalapeño, salt, and black pepper.

4 Crumble the cooked bacon and add to the bowl with the potatoes. Stir to combine and then scoop the mixture into a 4- to 6-quart (4- to 5.5-liter) slow cooker.

5 Cover and cook on low for 6 to 8 hours. Store in the refrigerator for up to 4 days.

VARIATION: If preferred, substitute 1 pound (450 grams) cooked sausage for the bacon.

TIP: Be sure to wear gloves when working with jalapeños! The oils can transfer to your hands and cause burning if you touch your face or eyes. Wash your hands well with dish soap after you've finished handling the pepper to remove the oils from your fingers.

Hearty Sausage & Potato Hash

Flavorful sausage and red potatoes combine for a hearty, savory breakfast that's both filling and satisfying. The juicy sausage drippings create potato bites bursting with bold sausage flavor!

YIELD	SERVING SIZE	PREP TIME	COOK TIME
6 CUPS	**1 CUP**	**10 MINUTES**	**5 TO 6 HOURS**

12 medium red potatoes (about 3lb [1.5kg]), cut into 1-inch (2.5cm) pieces

1 medium yellow onion, diced

½ tsp salt

¼ tsp freshly ground black pepper

¼ tsp dried oregano

¼ tsp dried basil

½ cup chicken broth

1lb (450g) whole fresh sausage in casings

1 Place the potatoes and onions in a 6- to 8-quart (5.5- to 7.5-liter) slow cooker. Add the salt, black pepper, oregano, basil, and chicken broth. Stir to combine.

2 Place the sausage on top of the potato mixture. Cover and cook on low for 5 to 6 hours.

3 When ready to serve, remove the sausage from the slow cooker. Cut the sausage into ¼-inch (6.5mm) slices, return the sausage to the slow cooker, and stir to combine. Serve hot. Store in the refrigerator for up to 4 days.

VARIATION: For a creamy, cheesy version, add 1 cup shredded cheddar cheese and ½ cup 2% milk during the last hour of cooking.

By the Way

Placing the potatoes in the bottom of the cooker gives them more contact with the heating element and helps them cook more quickly. A bonus of this layering is that the savory drippings from the sausage slowly smother the potatoes with extra flavor!

German Pancake

With only six ingredients and a short cooking time, this sweet egg pancake comes together with ease for a filling breakfast or brunch. The edges crisp in the butter for a caramelized, crusty crunch.

YIELD	SERVING SIZE	PREP TIME	COOK TIME
1 PANCAKE	**1 WEDGE**	**5 MINUTES**	**1 TO 2 HOURS**

3 tbsp butter, melted

6 large eggs

1 cup all-purpose flour

1 cup reduced fat (2%) milk

1 tsp pure vanilla extract

⅛ tsp salt

1 Pour the melted butter into a 6- to 8-quart (5.5- to 7.5-liter) slow cooker.

2 In a large bowl, whisk the eggs for 1 minute and then add the all-purpose flour, milk, vanilla extract, and salt. Continue whisking until well combined and few lumps remain.

3 Pour the batter into the buttered slow cooker. Cover and cook on high for 1 to 2 hours or until the center is set.

4 Slice into four wedges and serve topped with a dusting of confectioners' sugar, a drizzle of maple syrup, or fresh fruit.

VARIATION: For a different flavor twist, add 1 teaspoon ground cinnamon and a dash of nutmeg to the batter.

By the Way

When made using more traditional methods, pancakes will puff and then fall before serving. The low heat method and large size of this pancake doesn't produce the same impressive puff, but the end result is very much the same—and it tastes fantastic!

Cinnamon Swirl Coffee Cake

Soft and moist, with the zing of cinnamon, this coffee cake makes the perfect breakfast treat. The swirling ensures cinnamon flavor in every bite without being overly sweet.

YIELD	SERVING SIZE	PREP TIME	COOK TIME
10 SLICES	**1 SLICE**	**10 MINUTES**	**2½ TO 3 HOURS**

¾ cup butter, softened

1¾ cups sugar, divided

3 large eggs

1 tsp pure vanilla extract

2½ cups all-purpose flour

1 tsp baking soda

1 tsp baking powder

1 cup sour cream

1 tbsp ground cinnamon

1 Grease a 6- to 8-quart (5.5- to 7.5-liter) slow cooker with shortening, or spray with nonstick cooking spray.

2 In a large bowl, combine the butter and 1½ cups sugar. Use an electric mixer to beat the mixture on high for 2 minutes or until light and fluffy.

3 Add the eggs and continue to beat for about 1 minute or until blended.

4 Using a rubber spatula, stir in the vanilla extract, all-purpose flour, baking soda, baking powder, and sour cream. Continue stirring for about 1 minute or until the last of the flour is incorporated. (The batter will be very thick.)

5 Spoon half of the batter into the slow cooker and use the spatula to spread the mixture across the bottom of the insert.

6 In a small bowl, combine the remaining ¼ cup sugar with the cinnamon. Sprinkle the mixture over the batter. Spoon the remaining batter over the cinnamon mixture, spreading it as evenly as possible.

7 Insert a butter knife into the batter and move it around to swirl the cinnamon sugar into the batter, changing the direction of your pattern frequently to ensure all of the batter gets swirled.

8 Cover and cook on high for 2½ to 3 hours or until a toothpick or knife inserted into the middle of the cake comes out clean.

9 Invert the cake onto a serving platter. Serve warm or let cool before serving. Store in the refrigerator for up to 4 days.

By the Way

Coffee cakes are a bit of a misnomer as they are meant to be served with coffee, rather than contain coffee as an ingredient. Or perhaps it's just an excuse to have cake for breakfast!

French Toast Casserole

As this casserole cooks, the promise of cinnamon sugar and vanilla-soaked bread beckons you to the kitchen. The caramelized edges provide a special crispy treat.

YIELD	SERVING SIZE	PREP TIME	COOK TIME
8 SLICES	**1 SLICE**	**10 MINUTES**	**6 HOURS**

1 (16oz [450g]) loaf French bread, cut or torn into 1-inch (2.5cm) cubes

8oz (225g) cream cheese, diced

1 cup milk chocolate chips

2½ cups reduced fat (2%) milk

7 large eggs

1 cup heavy cream

½ cup firmly packed brown sugar (light or dark), divided

2 tsp pure vanilla extract

2 tsp ground cinnamon

4 tbsp butter, softened

1 Combine the bread cubes, cream cheese pieces, and chocolate chips in a 6- to 8-quart (5.5- to 7.5-liter) slow cooker. Toss to combine.

2 In a large bowl, combine the milk, eggs, and heavy cream. Whisk for about 2 minutes or until the eggs are incorporated.

3 Add ¼ cup of the brown sugar, vanilla extract, and cinnamon to the egg mixture. Whisk for 30 seconds. Pour the egg mixture over the bread mixture.

4 In a small bowl, stir together the remaining ¼ cup brown sugar and butter until a crumbly mixture forms. Sprinkle the crumble over the bread mixture.

5 Cover and cook on low for 6 hours.

6 Serve plain or topped with your favorite syrup. Store in the refrigerator for up to 4 days.

VARIATION: For a fall-inspired version, omit the chocolate chips and combine 1 cup pumpkin purée with the milk, eggs, and heavy cream.

TIP: If you want a less crispy crust, use an aluminum foil barrier.

Mexican Breakfast Casserole

This savory breakfast casserole is bursting with flavor. The green chiles, chili powder, crushed red pepper flakes, and pepper jack cheese combine for a mild spice and bold flavor that wakes you up and also fills you up.

YIELD	SERVING SIZE	PREP TIME	COOK TIME
2 CUPS	**1 CUP**	**20 MINUTES**	**8 HOURS**

1 lb (450g) fully cooked Mexican chorizo sausage, diced

1 (4oz [110g]) can diced green chiles, drained

1 medium white or yellow onion, diced

1 large red bell pepper, seeded, ribs removed, and diced

1 cup frozen corn kernels, thawed

10 large eggs

2 cups half & half

3 garlic cloves, crushed

2 tsp chili powder

½ tsp crushed red pepper flakes

½ tsp salt

½ tsp freshly ground black pepper

1½ cups shredded pepper jack cheese

1½ cups shredded cheddar cheese

20 (5½-inch [14cm]) corn tortillas

1 In a large bowl, stir together the chorizo, green chiles, onion, bell pepper, and corn.

2 In a separate large bowl, whisk together the eggs, half & half, garlic, chili powder, red pepper flakes, salt, and black pepper.

3 In a medium bowl, combine the pepper jack cheese and cheddar cheese.

4 Grease a 6- to 8-quart (5.5- to 7.5-liter) slow cooker with butter or shortening, or spray with nonstick cooking spray.

5 Cover the bottom of the slow cooker with 5 corn tortillas, tearing the tortillas, if necessary, to make them fit so they cover the entire bottom of the insert.

6 Spoon one third of the sausage-vegetable mixture onto the tortillas. Top with 1¾ cups of the egg mixture. Finish with ⅔ cup of the cheese mixture. Repeat the layering to create three layers and then top with a fourth layer of tortillas and the remaining 1 cup cheese mixture.

7 Cover and cook on low for 8 hours. Serve hot. Store in the refrigerator for up to 4 days.

TIP: Chorizo is a spicy sausage, and the Mexican variation of chorizo uses chili peppers and vinegar to create that spicy zing. If you can't find Mexican chorizo or Spanish chorizo in your grocery store, you can use any spicy sausage as a substitute.

Denver Omelet Casserole

Take breakfast back to a Colorado chuck wagon with the hearty flavors of this classic omelet. The hash brown crust adds a crunchy, filling bottom to the traditional ham, pepper, and onion–filled cheddar omelet flavors.

YIELD	SERVING SIZE	PREP TIME	COOK TIME
6 CUPS	**1 CUP**	**10 MINUTES**	**8 HOURS**

1 medium russet potato, peeled

12 large eggs

1 cup reduced fat (2%) milk

1 small yellow onion, diced

1 large green bell pepper, seeded, ribs removed, and diced

1 cup cooked ham, diced

1 cup shredded cheddar cheese

¼ tsp salt

⅛ tsp freshly ground black pepper

1 Using the largest grate on a box grater, shred the potato. Squeeze out any excess liquid and then place the potatoes in a 6- to 8-quart (5.5- to 7.5-liter) slow cooker.

2 In a large bowl, whisk the eggs and milk until well combined.

3 Stir in the yellow onion, green bell pepper, ham, cheddar cheese, salt, and black pepper.

4 Pour the mixture into the slow cooker. Cover and cook on low for 8 hours. Store in the refrigerator for up to 4 days.

By the Way

Omelets, frittatas, and quiches are all egg-based, but the differences in slow cooking these dishes comes in the ratio of eggs to liquid, which results in different consistencies. In this recipe, there's slightly more than 1 tablespoon of milk per egg. Frittatas have little, if any, added liquid. Quiches are richer and contain the highest amount of liquid-to-egg ratio.

Triple Cheese Sausage & Kale Frittata

Green kale and red sun-dried tomatoes provide a stunning presentation that matches the bold, bright flavors of this frittata. The combination of cheeses adds a sharp richness for a hearty breakfast that is sure to please.

YIELD	SERVING SIZE	PREP TIME	COOK TIME
2 CUPS	**1 CUP**	**15 MINUTES**	**8 HOURS**

1lb (450g) ground pork sausage

1 bunch kale, roughly chopped into 1-inch (2.5cm) pieces

10 large eggs

2 tbsp reduced fat (2%) milk

1 cup shredded provolone cheese

½ cup shredded mozzarella cheese

¼ cup grated Parmesan cheese

½ cup sun-dried tomatoes, roughly chopped

1 In a large skillet over medium-high heat, cook the pork sausage for about 6 to 8 minutes or until browned.

2 Add the kale, turn off the heat, and cover with a lid or aluminum foil. Let sit for 3 minutes.

3 Meanwhile, in a large bowl, whisk the eggs and milk until well combined.

4 Stir in the provolone cheese, mozzarella cheese, Parmesan cheese, and sun-dried tomatoes.

5 Stir the sausage and kale into the egg mixture and pour the mixture into a 6- to 8-quart (5.5- to 7.5-liter) slow cooker.

6 Cover and cook on low for 8 hours. Store in the refrigerator for up to 4 days.

VARIATION: You can easily switch up the cheese combinations in this recipe. Try Gruyère, goat cheese, and Parmesan; Gouda, sharp cheddar, and mozzarella; or provolone, Brie, and goat cheese.

TIP: Baby spinach is an acceptable substitution for the kale, but it should be added in with the egg mixture rather than pre-steaming it with the sausage.

By the Way

Kale is a tough, bitter leafy green that's chock full of vitamins and nutrients. In this recipe, the leaves are placed in with the sausage to steam a bit before they're added to the slow cooker. The steam helps soften the leaves to make them more palatable.

Spinach & Feta Quiche

In this savory quiche, feta and Parmesan cheeses add a sharp bite to the eggs, with just a hint of garlic. The slow cooking process leaves the quiche tender and moist on the inside, with a thin, crisp outer layer.

YIELD	SERVING SIZE	PREP TIME	COOK TIME
8 SLICES	**1 SLICE**	**5 MINUTES**	**6 TO 8 HOURS**

8 large eggs

2 cups reduced fat (2%) milk

2 cups fresh spinach leaves, loosely packed

2 garlic cloves, crushed

¾ cup crumbled feta cheese

½ cup grated Parmesan cheese

¼ tsp salt

¼ cup shredded mozzarella cheese

1 In a large bowl, whisk the eggs and milk until well combined.

2 Stir in the spinach leaves, garlic, feta cheese, Parmesan cheese, and salt.

3 Pour the mixture directly into a 6- to 8-quart (5.5- to 7.5-liter) slow cooker. Top with the mozzarella cheese.

4 Cover and cook on low for 6 to 8 hours. Store in the refrigerator for up to 4 days.

VARIATION: If desired, create a crunchy crust using thinly sliced potatoes. Overlap the slices slightly to cover the bottom and sides, reaching about 2 inches (5 centimeters) up the sides of the insert. The potatoes will get nice and crispy, and add a crunchy crust to the quiche.

Ham & Swiss Quiche

Don't be fooled by the simplicity of this recipe! The mild, nutty taste of the cheese melts in with the creamy eggs, while the salty ham balances out the decadence of this custard-like egg dish.

YIELD	SERVING SIZE	PREP TIME	COOK TIME
8 SLICES	**1 SLICE**	**10 MINUTES**	**8 HOURS**

8 large eggs

2 cups reduced fat (2%) milk

1 small yellow onion, diced

1 cup cooked ham steak, diced

1 cup shredded Swiss cheese

½ tsp salt

¼ tsp freshly ground black pepper

1 In a large bowl, whisk the eggs and milk until well combined.

2 Stir in the onions, ham, Swiss cheese, salt, and black pepper.

3 Pour the mixture into a 6- to 8-quart (5.5- to 7.5-liter) slow cooker.

4 Cover and cook on low for 8 hours. Store in the refrigerator for up to 4 days.

VARIATION: If desired, try different combinations of meat and cheese, such as bacon and cheddar, diced chicken and blue cheese, sausage and pepper jack, or pancetta and Gruyère.

TIP: Ham steak is a cooked slice of whole ham sold in the meat department of many grocery stores. If you can't find ham steak, you can substitute leftover baked ham or thick-sliced deli ham.

CHAPTER 3

Dips, Snacks, and More

Cooking with a slow cooker isn't just limited to meals. Low and slow also can produce some great snacks and other delights you might be surprised to find can be made in a slow cooker. Recipes like homemade yogurt or applesauce are super simple to make. A slow cooker also can be a handy helper for parties, when you might need to prepare dishes several hours in advance.

Note that you will see varying sizes of slow cookers listed in the recipes in this chapter because dips and appetizers tend to be made in smaller amounts.

Spinach Artichoke Dip

This classic dip, featuring a creamy combination of artichoke hearts and spinach, is always a party favorite. Basil and garlic add subtle flavors to enhance the mild taste of the artichokes.

YIELD	SERVING SIZE	PREP TIME	COOK TIME
4 CUPS	**¼ CUP**	**5 MINUTES**	**2 TO 3 HOURS**

10oz (285g) frozen spinach, thawed and drained

8oz (225g) cream cheese

¼ cup mayonnaise

½ cup grated Parmesan cheese

1 garlic clove, crushed

½ tsp dried basil

¼ tsp salt

¼ tsp freshly ground black pepper

14oz (400g) jar artichoke hearts, drained and roughly chopped

¾ cup shredded mozzarella cheese, divided

1 Using your hands, squeeze as much liquid from the spinach as possible. Set aside.

2 Lightly grease a 2- or 3-quart (2- or 3-liter) slow cooker with butter, shortening, or vegetable oil, or spray with nonstick cooking spray.

3 In a large bowl, combine the cream cheese, mayonnaise, Parmesan cheese, garlic, basil, salt, black pepper, artichoke hearts, spinach, and ½ cup of the mozzarella cheese.

4 Spread the mixture in the slow cooker and top with the remaining ¼ cup mozzarella cheese.

5 Cover and cook on high for 2 to 3 hours.

6 Serve hot with bread or tortilla chips. Store in an airtight container in the refrigerator for up to 4 days.

VARIATION: For even more flavor, add 5 ounces (140 grams) chopped sun-dried tomatoes.

TIP: You can easily thaw frozen spinach in the microwave. Simply heat on high for 1 minute and stir. Repeat until the spinach is completely thawed.

Southwestern Cheesy Corn Dip

Sweet red bell pepper and corn are paired with a hint of heat from jalapeño in this creamy corn salsa. Served hot as a dip, it's a fun appetizer that features a zesty southwestern flavor.

YIELD	SERVING SIZE	PREP TIME	COOK TIME
3 CUPS	**¼ CUP**	**5 MINUTES**	**2 TO 3 HOURS**

1 tbsp butter, melted

2 cups frozen corn kernels, thawed

½ small yellow onion, diced

1 large red bell pepper, seeded, ribs removed, and diced

2 green onions (green parts only), sliced

1 jalapeño, seeded, ribs removed, and finely diced

1 garlic clove, crushed

¼ cup mayonnaise

½ cup shredded Monterey Jack cheese

½ cup shredded cheddar cheese

1 Lightly grease a 2- or 3-quart (2- or 3-liter) slow cooker with butter, shortening, or vegetable oil, or spray with nonstick cooking spray.

2 In a large bowl, stir together the melted butter, corn, onion, red bell peppers, green onions, jalapeño, garlic, mayonnaise, Monterey Jack cheese, and cheddar cheese. Spread the mixture into the slow cooker.

3 Cover and cook on high for 2 to 3 hours.

4 Serve hot with tortilla chips or sliced bread. Store in an airtight container in the refrigerator for up to 4 days.

VARIATION: For a spicier dip, add additional jalapeños, or substitute a hotter pepper, like a serrano.

TIP: To clean the green onions, remove the bands holding the bunch together and discard any wilted leaves. Using a sharp knife, trim off the stringy roots and slice the onions about ⅛ inch (3 millimeters) thick.

Chile Con Queso

Warm and gooey, with a kick of heat, this Mexican bean dip is packed full of flavor. A bowlful is simple yet satisfying, with bites of cheesy beans, bell peppers, and onions.

YIELD	SERVING SIZE	PREP TIME	COOK TIME
6 CUPS	**½ CUP**	**10 MINUTES**	**5 HOURS**

15oz (420g) can black beans, drained and rinsed

15oz (420g) can kidney beans, drained and rinsed

15oz (420g) can diced tomatoes, drained

4oz (110g) can diced green chiles, drained

6oz (170g) can tomato paste

2 large red bell peppers, seeded, ribs removed, and diced

1 large yellow onion, diced

4 garlic cloves, crushed

1 tbsp chili powder

2½ cups shredded cheddar cheese

8oz (225g) cream cheese

1 Lightly grease a 4- to 6-quart (4- to 5.5-liter) slow cooker with butter, shortening, or vegetable oil, or spray with nonstick cooking spray.

2 In the slow cooker, combine the black beans, kidney beans, tomatoes, green chiles, tomato paste, red bell peppers, onions, garlic, and chili powder.

3 Cover and cook on high for 4 hours.

4 Stir in the cheddar cheese and cream cheese.

5 Cover and cook on high for 1 more hour.

6 Stir before serving. Serve hot with tortilla chips on the side. Store in an airtight container in the refrigerator for up to 4 days.

VARIATION: For a spicier flavor, add a minced jalapeño or serrano pepper.

By the Way

Chile con queso translates to "chile with cheese." The dish originates in northern Mexico and has made its way into the heart of Tex-Mex cuisine. It's most often eaten as a dip, but it also can be used as a condiment. This particular recipe is quite hearty, thanks to the vegetables and beans.

Buffalo Chicken Dip

The spicy kick of buffalo chicken wings is transformed into a simple dip that's always a party favorite. Traditional buffalo wing ingredients give this addicting dip a classic flavor and a cool, rich, and velvety feel.

YIELD	SERVING SIZE	PREP TIME	COOK TIME
4 CUPS	**¼ CUP**	**5 MINUTES**	**6 HOURS**

2lb (1kg) boneless, skinless chicken breasts, trimmed

1½ cups buffalo wing sauce, divided

16oz (450g) cream cheese

½ cup blue cheese dressing

½ cup ranch dressing

2 cups shredded cheddar cheese

1 In a 2- or 3-quart (2- or 3-liter) slow cooker, add the chicken breasts and pour 1 cup of the wing sauce over the top.

2 Cover and cook on high for 4 hours.

3 When the cook time is complete, use forks to shred the chicken and then drain any excess liquid from the mixture. Stir in the cream cheese, blue cheese dressing, ranch dressing, and cheddar cheese.

4 Cover and cook on high for 2 more hours.

5 Serve hot with tortilla chips, sliced baguettes, carrot sticks, or celery sticks. Store in the refrigerator for up to 4 days.

TIP: If you're short on time, you can replace the fresh chicken breasts with 2 (10oz [285g]) cans of cooked chicken that have been drained. Skip the precooking in steps 1 and 2, add the canned chicken to the slow cooker in step 3, and cook the dip for 2 hours on high.

Roasted Red Pepper Dip

Sweet roasted red bell peppers are the star of this creamy recipe.
Parmesan adds a slight sharpness, and paprika enhances the
natural flavors of the bell peppers to create a versatile dip.

YIELD	SERVING SIZE	PREP TIME	COOK TIME
3 CUPS	**¼ CUP**	**5 MINUTES**	**2 TO 3 HOURS**

2 (12oz [340g]) jars roasted
red bell peppers, drained
and roughly chopped

½ cup shredded
Parmesan cheese

1 cup shredded
mozzarella cheese

8oz (225g) cream cheese

2 tsp ground paprika

2 garlic cloves, peeled
and crushed

1 Lightly grease a 2- or 3-quart (2- or 3-liter) slow cooker with butter, shortening, or vegetable oil, or spray with nonstick cooking spray.

2 Add the red bell peppers, Parmesan cheese, mozzarella cheese, cream cheese, paprika, and garlic to the slow cooker. Stir to combine.

3 Cover and cook on high for 2 to 3 hours.

4 Serve hot with bread or tortilla chips. Store in the refrigerator for up to 4 days.

By the Way

Paprika is created by grinding red bell peppers and chili peppers, and adding it to recipes helps bring out the natural sweet and slightly spicy flavors of bell peppers. Many grocery stores sell paprika labeled as simply "paprika" or "ground paprika." You might also find "sweet paprika" or "smoked paprika." The differences come from the preparation of the peppers and result in subtle variations in intensity and sweetness.

Cheese Fondue

Fondue is a party favorite and always perfect for serving a crowd.
In this recipe, pieces of hearty bread or crisp vegetables are dunked
in melted cheese for an ooey-gooey culinary experience.

YIELD	SERVING SIZE	PREP TIME	COOK TIME
1 CUP	**¼ CUP**	**5 MINUTES**	**1½ TO 2 HOURS**

¼ cup shredded
cheddar cheese

¼ cup shredded
Swiss cheese

5oz (140g) plain
goat cheese

¼ cup white wine

⅛ tsp ground nutmeg

Crusty bread or crunchy
vegetables, such as
carrots or celery, for
dipping

1 Add the cheddar cheese, Swiss cheese, goat cheese, white wine, and nutmeg to a 1- or 2-quart (1- or 2-liter) slow cooker. Stir to combine.

2 Cover and cook on low for 1½ to 2 hours or until the cheeses are completely melted, and then immediately reduce the cooker setting to warm.

3 Keep the cooker on warm while serving the fondue with the bread or vegetables. Store in the refrigerator for up to 4 days.

VARIATION: Any combination of melting cheeses will work in this recipe. Feel free to substitute ¼ cup each of any three of your favorite cheeses.

TIP: Alcohol does not burn off in the slow cooking process, so if you need an alcohol-free version of this recipe, you can substitute an equal amount of grape or apple juice for the white wine.

Baba Ghanoush

This traditional Middle Eastern dip combines the creamy texture of eggplant, the sweet flavor of roasted garlic, and the nutty flavor of sesame seeds from the tahini paste. Lemon juice adds a tangy brightness to this flavorful spread.

YIELD	SERVING SIZE	PREP TIME	COOK TIME
2 CUPS	**¼ CUP**	**5 MINUTES**	**2 TO 3 HOURS**

1 large eggplant

1 head of garlic

1 tbsp olive oil

Juice of 1 medium lemon

¼ cup tahini paste

½ tsp salt

2 tbsp chopped fresh parsley

1 Using a fork, pierce the outside of the eggplant at least a dozen times over the entire surface. Place the eggplant in a 4- to 6-quart (4- to 5.5-liter) slow cooker.

2 Cut the pointed end off the head of garlic, exposing the cloves. Drizzle the head with olive oil and then wrap in aluminum foil. Place the wrapped garlic in the slow cooker.

3 Cover and cook on high for 2 to 3 hours.

4 Remove the eggplant and garlic from the slow cooker. Cut the eggplant in half lengthwise and use a large spoon to scoop out the flesh. Place in a blender or a food processor fitted with an S blade.

5 Gently squeeze the garlic cloves out of their peels and into the food processor or blender. Add the lemon juice, tahini paste, and salt. Purée for about 1 minute or until smooth.

6 Cover and refrigerate for 2 hours. When ready to serve, sprinkle with the parsley. Serve cold with pita chips or pita bread. Store in the refrigerator for up to 4 days.

VARIATION: For a Mediterranean twist, add ¼ cup chopped sun-dried tomatoes or ¼ cup chopped black olives. Or, for an Egyptian twist, add 1 diced medium tomato, ½ cup diced white onion, ½ teaspoon cumin, and ½ teaspoon chili powder.

Homemade Yogurt

You can enjoy the creamy goodness of homemade yogurt by making your own at home in a slow cooker. It's so easy to make, and you can create your own fruit-flavored versions simply by adding any crushed fruit!

YIELD	SERVING SIZE	PREP TIME	COOK TIME
6 CUPS	**½ CUP**	**5 MINUTES**	**8 HOURS**

8 cups whole milk

½ cup plain yogurt with
   live cultures

1 Add the milk to a 6- to 8-quart (5.5- to 7.5-liter) slow cooker.

2 Cover and cook on high for 1 hour and then unplug the slow cooker and let the milk sit, covered, for 30 minutes.

3 Stir in the plain yogurt, cover again, and wrap the entire slow cooker in a large bath or beach towel. Let the mixture sit undisturbed for 8 to 12 hours.

4 Remove the towel and refrigerate as is or thicken the yogurt by straining it through cheesecloth to remove the whey.

5 Store in an airtight container in the refrigerator for up to 1 month.

VARIATION: For **Homemade Vanilla Yogurt,** stir in ¼ cup sugar, honey, or other sweetener, and 2 teaspoons pure vanilla extract.

By the Way

Using a store-bought yogurt that contains live cultures is the simplest way to gain a starter. For future batches, simply save ½ cup of your homemade yogurt to use as a starter.

Ultimate Cranberry Sauce

The sweetness of the sugars combines with the tartness of the cranberries to produce a delicious and delightful cranberry sauce with a zing. The orange juice provides a punch of citrus to balance out the flavors.

YIELD	SERVING SIZE	PREP TIME	COOK TIME
2 CUPS	**¼ CUP**	**5 MINUTES**	**2 HOURS**

3 cups fresh cranberries

½ cup orange juice

½ cup brown sugar (light or dark), firmly packed

½ cup sugar

1 Combine the cranberries, orange juice, brown sugar, and sugar in a 2- to 4-quart (2- to 4-liter) slow cooker.

2 Cover and cook on high for 2 hours.

3 Transfer the sauce to a blender, filling the blender pitcher no more than half full. Place the lid securely on the pitcher and loosen the removable fill cap to create a vent for the steam. Purée until smooth. (Note: Pressure buildup can lead to explosions, so always be sure to vent any steam while puréeing.)

4 Serve hot or cold. Store in an airtight container in the refrigerator for up to 4 days.

VARIATION: For a spicy sauce, add 1 diced jalapeño that has had the ribs and seeds removed. Or, for a double berry sauce, add 2 cups fresh raspberries.

TIP: Fresh cranberries should be firm or hard. If you find any soft berries in the batch, discard them.

By the Way

Cranberries are harvested during the fall months in North America. From September to November, the fields are flooded and special harvesters knock the berries loose. The cranberries then float to the top of the water and are skimmed or pumped out.

Cinnamon Brown Sugar Applesauce

Cinnamon and brown sugar give this traditional applesauce a dark color and rich flavor, and create a delectably sweet and spiced apple purée.

YIELD	SERVING SIZE	PREP TIME	COOK TIME
6 CUPS	**½ CUP**	**30 MINUTES**	**8 HOURS**

5lb (2.5kg) apples, peeled, cored, and sliced

½ cup apple juice

½ cup brown sugar (light or dark), firmly packed

1 tbsp ground cinnamon

½ tsp ground cloves

½ tsp ground nutmeg

1 Layer the apple slices into the bottom of a 6- to 8-quart (5.5- to 7.5-liter) slow cooker.

2 Pour in the apple juice and then stir in the brown sugar, cinnamon, cloves, and nutmeg.

3 Cover and cook on low for 8 hours.

4 Using a potato masher, mash any remaining apple chunks for a chunky-style applesauce, or transfer the mixture to a blender or a food processor fitted with an S blade to purée until smooth. Store in the refrigerator for up to 4 days.

VARIATION: For plain, sugar-free applesauce, substitute water for the apple juice and omit the brown sugar and spices.

TIP: An apple peeler/corer/slicer makes prepping the apples quick and easy. If you don't have one, you can use a vegetable peeler to peel the apples and then core and slice them using a knife.

By the Way

The best applesauce comes from a mixture of multiple types of apples, rather than just relying on one kind of apple. I recommend using any combination of McIntosh, Golden Delicious, Granny Smith, Fuji, or Jonathan apples.

Homemade Strawberry Jam

Enjoy the sweet berry goodness of your own fresh, homemade, strawberry jam. Spread it over toast or bagels, or use it to create your lunchtime peanut butter and jelly sandwich. Homemade jam is an absolute treat!

YIELD	SERVING SIZE	PREP TIME	COOK TIME
6 CUPS	**2 TABLESPOONS**	**30 MINUTES**	**6 TO 8 HOURS**

4lb (2kg) fresh strawberries, hulled and sliced

2 tbsp lemon juice

6 cups sugar

4½ tbsp pectin

1 Add the strawberries, lemon juice, sugar, and pectin to a 6- to 8-quart (5.5- to 7.5-liter) slow cooker.

2 Cover and cook on low for 6 to 8 hours.

3 Using a potato masher, mash the strawberries for a chunky jam. Or transfer in batches to a blender or a food processor fitted with an S blade to purée for a smooth jam.

4 Store in an airtight container in the refrigerator for up to 1 month or freeze in resealable plastic freezer bags for up to 9 months

VARIATIONS: For **Homemade Apricot Jam,** use 4 pounds (2 kilograms) apricots, pitted, peeled, and sliced; ¼ cup lemon juice; 4 cups sugar; and 4½ tablespoons pectin. For **Homemade Peach Jam,** use 4 pounds (2 kilograms) peaches, peeled; ¼ cup lemon juice; 4 cups sugar; and 4½ tablespoons pectin. For **Homemade Blackberry Jam**, use 4 cups blackberries; 2 tablespoons lemon juice; 5 cups sugar; and 4½ tablespoons pectin. For **Homemade Raspberry Jam,** use 4 cups raspberries; 2 tablespoons lemon juice; 5 cups sugar; and 4½ tablespoons pectin.

By the Way

Pectin is a natural thickening agent. You can find it in almost any grocery store in the baking or canning aisle.

Apple-Pumpkin Butter

In this sweet, spiced, and condensed butter, the apples and pumpkins reduce, and the flavors concentrate, to produce a rich and satisfying combination that features the flavors of cinnamon, cloves, nutmeg, and ginger.

YIELD	SERVING SIZE	PREP TIME	COOK TIME
6 CUPS	**2 TABLESPOONS**	**30 MINUTES**	**8 HOURS**

5lb (2.5kg) apples, peeled, cored, and sliced

2 cups pumpkin purée

¼ cup apple juice

Juice of 1 medium lemon

1 cup sugar

2 tbsp ground cinnamon

1 tsp ground cloves

1 tsp ground nutmeg

1 tsp ground ginger

1 Add the apple slices and pumpkin purée to a 6- to 8-quart (5.5- to 7.5-liter) slow cooker.

2 Pour in the apple juice and then add the lemon juice, sugar, cinnamon, cloves, nutmeg, and ginger. Stir well to combine.

3 Cover and cook on low for 8 hours.

4 Transfer the apple-pumpkin butter to a blender, filling the blender pitcher no more than half full. Place the lid securely on the pitcher and loosen the removable fill cap to create a vent for the steam. Purée for 1 to 2 minutes or until smooth. (Note: Pressure buildup can lead to explosions, so always be sure to vent any steam while puréeing.) Alternatively, you can use an immersion blender to purée the apple-pumpkin butter in the slow cooker.

5 Store in an airtight container in the refrigerator for up to 1 month or freeze in resealable plastic freezer bags for up to 9 months.

VARIATION: For **Apple-Fig Butter,** replace the pumpkin purée with 2 cups dried figs, stems removed.

TIP: Different varieties of apples produce slightly different results. Granny Smith or other tart varieties give a more acidic bite, while sweeter varieties like Red Delicious produce a more sugary butter.

By the Way

This butter is terrific for use on toast, pancakes, sandwiches, or even as a sweet glaze for meats.

Homemade Ketchup

Replace that commercially prepared bottled ketchup with your own homemade version using this simple recipe. You'll be pleasantly surprised by the bold flavors that will turn ketchup into a whole new experience.

YIELD	SERVING SIZE	PREP TIME	COOK TIME
2 CUPS	**1 CUP**	**10 MINUTES**	**8 HOURS**

4lb (2kg) Roma tomatoes, cored and diced

1 small yellow onion, diced

⅔ cup apple cider vinegar

¼ cup brown sugar (light or dark), firmly packed

2 tsp salt

½ tsp dry mustard powder

½ tsp crushed red pepper flakes

¼ tsp ground cinnamon

¼ tsp ground allspice

¼ tsp ground nutmeg

¼ tsp ground ginger

⅛ tsp ground cloves

1 Add the tomatoes and onions to a 6- to 8-quart (5.5- to 7.5-liter) slow cooker.

2 Pour in the apple cider vinegar and stir in the brown sugar, salt, dry mustard, crushed red pepper flakes, cinnamon, allspice, nutmeg, ginger, and cloves.

3 Cover and cook on low for 8 hours.

4 In small batches, carefully transfer the ketchup to a blender, filling the blender pitcher no more than half full for each batch. Place the lid securely on the pitcher and loosen the removable fill cap to create a vent for the steam. Purée in batches until smooth, and then strain the ketchup through a fine mesh strainer to remove any excess liquid. (Note: Pressure buildup can lead to explosions, so always be sure to vent any steam while puréeing.)

5 Store in an airtight container in the refrigerator for up to 1 month.

VARIATION: For an Asian flavor, replace the apple cider vinegar with rice wine vinegar and add 1 tablespoon soy sauce and ½ teaspoon sesame seeds.

TIP: For a smoother-textured ketchup, remove the tomato skins before dicing. For easier dicing, bring a large pot of water to a boil over high heat. Add the tomatoes and blanch for 30 to 60 seconds, then use tongs to immediately transfer the tomatoes to a large bowl filled with ice water. Once the skins begin to crack and peel, you can use your fingers to pull away the skins.

Tomato Bacon Chutney

This chutney packs a powerful punch of flavor, thanks to smoky bacon, acidic tomatoes, and fragrant rosemary. Your taste buds will love the complex flavors of this tasty treat!

YIELD	SERVING SIZE	PREP TIME	COOK TIME
4 CUPS	**¼ CUP**	**20 MINUTES**	**3½ TO 4 HOURS**

1½lb (680g) sliced bacon, diced

2 large yellow onions, diced

5 garlic cloves, peeled and minced

½ cup apple cider vinegar

½ cup brown sugar (light or dark), firmly packed

¼ cup honey

2 (15oz [420g]) cans diced tomatoes, drained

2 tsp ground paprika

1 tsp dried rosemary

¼ tsp salt

¼ tsp freshly ground black pepper

1 In a large skillet over medium-high heat, cook the bacon, flipping every 60 seconds, for 12 to 15 minutes or until crispy. Transfer the cooked bacon to a paper towel-lined plate to drain.

2 Combine the bacon, onions, garlic, apple cider vinegar, brown sugar, honey, tomatoes, paprika, rosemary, salt, and black pepper in a 6- to 8-quart (5.5- to 7.5-liter) slow cooker.

3 Cover and cook on high for 3½ to 4 hours.

4 Serve as either a hot or cold condiment. Store in an airtight container in the refrigerator for up to 2 weeks.

TIP: Measuring honey can get a bit sticky. To help the honey pour right out, spray your measuring cup with nonstick cooking spray before measuring the honey.

CHAPTER 4

Soups, Stews, and Chilis

Low and slow is the perfect way to cook soups, stews, and chilis. Instead of tending a pot over a hot stove for what can sometimes be hours, the slow cooker does the work for you, making it the perfect tool for creating soups, stews, and chilis.

Tomato Bisque

A hot bowl of tomato soup is the perfect comfort food on a cold and rainy day. Sweet, acidic tomatoes are paired with basil and garlic in this warm and satisfying soup.

YIELD	SERVING SIZE	PREP TIME	COOK TIME
8 CUPS	**1 CUP**	**15 MINUTES**	**6 TO 8 HOURS**

4lb (2kg) Roma tomatoes, cored and diced

1 medium yellow onion, diced

2 medium carrots, peeled and diced

2 medium celery ribs, sliced

4 garlic cloves, minced

1 tsp dried basil

1½ tsp salt

¼ tsp freshly ground black pepper

2 cups chicken broth

1 cup heavy cream

1 Add the tomatoes, onion, carrots, celery, garlic, basil, salt, black pepper, and chicken broth to a 6- to 8-quart (5.5- to 7.5-liter) slow cooker.

2 Cover and cook on low for 6 to 8 hours.

3 Working in small batches, carefully transfer the soup to a blender. Fill the blender pitcher no more than half full for each batch, place the lid securely on the pitcher, and loosen the removable fill cap to create a vent for the steam. Purée in batches for 1 to 2 minutes or until smooth. (Note: Pressure buildup can lead to explosions, so always be sure to vent any steam while puréeing.)

4 Stir in the heavy cream before serving. Store in the refrigerator for up to 4 days.

VARIATION: For a spicier soup, add 1 teaspoon crushed red pepper flakes.

TIP: If you don't have a blender or food processor, you can use an immersion blender to purée the soup right in the slow cooker.

Comforting Corn Chowder

This creamy chowder is refreshingly light, yet filling enough
to be a meal. Sweet corn is combined with mild potatoes, celery,
and sharp onion for a warm, comforting, creamy soup.

YIELD	SERVING SIZE	PREP TIME	COOK TIME
12 CUPS	**2 CUPS**	**10 MINUTES**	**4½ TO 6½ HOURS**

4 cups frozen corn kernels, thawed

3 medium russet potatoes, peeled and cut into 1-inch (2.5cm) pieces

1 medium yellow onion, diced

5 medium celery stalks, sliced

2 tbsp sugar

2 tsp salt

2 cups chicken broth

3 cups half & half

1 Add the corn, potatoes, onion, and celery to a 6- to 8-quart (5.5- to 7.5-liter) slow cooker.

2 Sprinkle the sugar and salt over the vegetables and then pour in the chicken broth. Stir to combine.

3 Cover and cook on low for 4 to 6 hours and then pour in the half & half, increase the heat to high, and cook for 30 more minutes.

4 Store in the refrigerator for up to 4 days.

VARIATION: For **Chicken Corn Chowder,** trim and cut 2 pounds (1kg) boneless, skinless chicken breasts into 1-inch (2.5cm) cubes, and add at the same time as the corn, potatoes, onion, and celery.

TIP: You can use fresh, canned, or frozen corn in this recipe. If you opt for fresh, 1 ear of corn will yield approximately ½ cup corn kernels. If you opt for canned corn, use a 16-ounce (450g) can. (Drain the liquid from the can before using.)

Green Chile Pork Stew

In this rich and hearty stew, tender, slow-simmered pork is combined with the Mexican flavors of cumin, garlic, and green chile, while cayenne offers a spicy kick.

YIELD	SERVING SIZE	PREP TIME	COOK TIME
12 CUPS	**2 CUPS**	**15 MINUTES**	**6 TO 8 HOURS**

2 medium russet potatoes, peeled and cut into 1-inch (2.5cm) cubes

3 medium carrots, peeled and diced

1 medium yellow onion, diced

1 large tomato, diced

3 garlic cloves, crushed

2lb (1kg) boneless pork loin roast, trimmed and cut into 1-inch (2.5cm) cubes

1½ tsp salt

1 tsp dried oregano

1 tsp ground cumin

½ tsp freshly ground black pepper

½ tsp cayenne

1 bay leaf

4 cups chicken broth

10oz (285g) can whole green chiles, drained and roughly chopped

1 Layer the potatoes, carrots, and onion in a 6- to 8-quart (5.5- to 7.5-liter) slow cooker. Top with the tomato and garlic, and then place the pork loin roast on top of the vegetables.

2 Season with the salt, oregano, cumin, black pepper, and cayenne, and then add the bay leaf. Pour the chicken broth over the meat and vegetables.

3 Cover and cook on low for 6 to 8 hours.

4 Remove the bay leaf and stir in the green chiles before serving. Store in the refrigerator for up to 4 days.

By the Way

Because canned green chiles are already cooked in the canning process, additional long, slow cooking can dilute the flavor. This stew highlights the green chiles, so you'll want to add them at the end of the cooking process so they provide the most flavor.

Creamy Broccoli Cheese Soup

Broccoli is the star of this rich and creamy soup that's loaded with fresh broccoli, savory onion, and gooey cheddar cheese.

YIELD	SERVING SIZE	PREP TIME	COOK TIME
12 CUPS	**2 CUPS**	**10 MINUTES**	**3 TO 4 HOURS**

4 cups broccoli florets (about 2 medium bunches)

1 medium yellow onion, diced

4 garlic cloves, minced

4 cups half & half

2 cups reduced fat (2%) milk

1½ tsp salt

3 cups shredded cheddar cheese

1 Add the broccoli, onion, garlic, half & half, milk, and salt to a 6- to 8-quart (5.5- to 7.5-liter) slow cooker. Stir to combine.

2 Cover and cook on low for 3 to 4 hours.

3 Add the cheddar cheese and stir until melted. Store in the refrigerator for up to 4 days.

VARIATION: For a smoky flavor, add cooked and crumbled bacon just before serving.

TIP: For a more developed flavor, sauté the onions in 1 tablespoon olive oil in a skillet over medium-high heat for 5 to 7 minutes before adding them to the slow cooker.

By the Way

Because broccoli can cook rather quickly and end up mushy if overcooked, this soup has a shorter cooking time than most soups in this chapter. This shorter cooking time also allows for the use of milk and half & half, which can curdle if cooked at high heat.

Indian-Style Spiced Chili

The spicy flavors of India meet American chili in this unusual and delightful twist on traditional chili. Garam masala and cinnamon impart exotic flavors, while heavy cream adds a creamy element.

YIELD	SERVING SIZE	PREP TIME	COOK TIME
12 CUPS	**2 CUPS**	**10 MINUTES**	**6 TO 8 HOURS**

2lb (1kg) boneless, skinless chicken breasts, trimmed and cut into 1-inch (2.5cm) cubes

15oz (420g) can chickpeas, drained and rinsed

15oz (420g) can kidney beans, drained and rinsed

1 medium yellow onion, diced

1 jalapeño, stemmed, seeded, and minced

2 tsp paprika

2 tsp garam masala

1 tsp ground cumin

½ tsp ground cinnamon

½ tsp salt

⅛ tsp ground turmeric

8oz (225g) can tomato sauce

1 cup chicken broth

1 cup whipping cream

1 Add the chicken, chickpeas, kidney beans, onion, and jalapeño to a 6- to 8-quart (5.5- to 7.5-liter) slow cooker.

2 Stir in the paprika, garam masala, cumin, cinnamon, salt, and ground turmeric. Pour in the tomato sauce and chicken broth. Stir to combine.

3 Cover and cook on low for 6 to 8 hours.

4 Stir in the whipping cream just before serving. Store in the refrigerator for up to 4 days.

By the Way

Garam masala is an Indian spice blend of cumin, coriander, cardamom, black pepper, cinnamon, cloves, and nutmeg. The whole spices are toasted and ground into a distinctly flavorful mixture. You can find garam masala in the spice sections of most grocery stores.

Old-Fashioned Beef Stew

Tender chunks of beef slowly simmer with potatoes, carrots, and celery in this thick and hearty stew. Pearl onions and herbs add to the depth of flavor.

YIELD	SERVING SIZE	PREP TIME	COOK TIME
12 CUPS	**2 CUPS**	**15 MINUTES**	**8 TO 10 HOURS**

2 tbsp vegetable oil

2lb (1kg) beef stew meat, cubed

2 tbsp cornstarch

8 medium red potatoes, cut into 1-inch (2.5cm) chunks

1lb (450g) pearl or boiling onions, peeled

4 medium carrots, peeled and sliced

4 medium celery stalks, sliced

2 garlic cloves, minced

1 tsp salt

1 tsp sugar

½ tsp freshly ground black pepper

½ tsp dried rosemary

½ tsp dried parsley

½ tsp paprika

¼ tsp dried oregano

¼ tsp dried basil

¼ tsp ground allspice

2 cups beef broth

2 tbsp Worcestershire sauce

1 bay leaf

1 Heat the vegetable oil in a large skillet over medium-high heat. Add the stew meat and sear for about 2 minutes per side.

2 Dust the meat with the cornstarch. Cook for 1 more minute to sear the cornstarch into meat and then transfer to a 6- to 8-quart (5.5- to 7.5-liter) slow cooker.

3 Add the potatoes, onions, carrots, celery, and garlic. Season with the salt, sugar, black pepper, rosemary, parsley, paprika, oregano, basil, and allspice.

4 Pour in the beef broth and add the Worcestershire sauce. Stir briefly to combine and then tuck the bay leaf down into the liquid.

5 Cover and cook on low for 8 to 10 hours.

6 Remove the bay leaf before serving. Store in the refrigerator for up to 4 days.

TIP: If you can't find pearl onions, you can use 1 medium yellow or white onion, peeled and diced.

By the Way

Cornstarch is often used as a thickening agent in soups and stews, but you can't just dump cornstarch into a liquid or you'll end up with clumps of cornstarch floating in the soup. Instead, the cornstarch needs to bond with some sort of fat. In this recipe, the cornstarch bonds with both the meat and the olive oil, allowing it to spread evenly throughout the soup and thicken the liquid as it cooks. Flour is another common thickening agent.

Chicken Taco Soup

Loaded with beans, tomatoes, onions, and chiles, this soup contains everything a taco has to offer, and it's all in a convenient, hearty, and filling soup.

YIELD	SERVING SIZE	PREP TIME	COOK TIME
12 CUPS	**2 CUPS**	**15 MINUTES**	**6 TO 8 HOURS**

2lb (1kg) boneless, skinless chicken breasts, trimmed and cut into 1-inch (2.5cm) cubes

1 medium yellow onion, diced

2 garlic cloves, crushed

1 cup frozen corn kernels, thawed

15oz (420g) can pinto beans, drained and rinsed

15oz (420g) can kidney beans, drained and rinsed

2 (15oz [420g]) cans diced tomatoes, with liquid

2 (4oz [110g]) cans diced green chiles, with liquid

2 tsp paprika

1½ tsp salt

1 tsp chili powder

1 tsp dried oregano

1 tsp ground cumin

½ tsp crushed red pepper flakes

6 cups chicken broth

Juice of 1 medium lime

1 Add the chicken breasts to a 6- to 8-quart (5.5- to 7.5-liter) slow cooker.

2 Add the onion, garlic, corn, pinto beans, kidney beans, tomatoes, green chiles, paprika, salt, chili powder, oregano, cumin, crushed red pepper flakes, and chicken broth. Stir to combine.

3 Cover and cook on low for 6 to 8 hours.

4 Stir in the lime juice before serving. Store in the refrigerator for up to 4 days.

VARIATION: For **Beef Taco Soup,** substitute 2 pounds (1 kilogram) browned and drained ground beef for the chicken.

TIP: Toppings aren't necessary with this soup, but a dollop of sour cream, a sprinkle of shredded cheddar cheese, and chopped fresh green onions or cilantro will provide an extra layer of flavor.

By the Way

Before using canned beans in a recipe, always drain and rinse them, unless otherwise directed. Beans are canned in a thick, starchy liquid that can discolor your slow cooker insert. The liquid also contains sodium, which may lead to an overly salty recipe.

Slow Braised Sweet Pork Chili

Tangy pineapple and sweet apple juice combine with savory flavors and spices in this beautifully balanced sweet pork chili.

YIELD	SERVING SIZE	PREP TIME	COOK TIME
12 CUPS	**2 CUPS**	**15 MINUTES**	**8 TO 10 HOURS**

2lb (1kg) pork roast, trimmed and cut into 1-inch (2.5cm) cubes

1 medium yellow bell pepper, stemmed, ribs and seeds removed, and diced

3 cups cubed fresh pineapple (about 1 medium)

15oz (420g) can black beans, drained and rinsed

2 cups frozen corn kernels, thawed

6oz (170g) can tomato paste

3 medium tomatoes, diced

1 cup sliced green onions (about 1 bunch)

4 garlic cloves, minced

3 tbsp brown sugar (light or dark)

1 tbsp paprika

2 tsp salt

½ tsp freshly ground black pepper

½ tsp chili powder

¼ tsp ground cinnamon

1¼ cups apple juice

1 tbsp apple cider vinegar

1 Add the pork roast, yellow bell pepper, pineapple, black beans, corn, tomato paste, tomatoes, green onions, and garlic to a 6- to 8-quart (5.5- to 7.5-liter) slow cooker.

2 Sprinkle in the brown sugar, paprika, salt, black pepper, chili powder, and cinnamon. Pour in the apple juice and add the apple cider vinegar. Stir to combine.

3 Cover and cook on low for 8 to 10 hours.

4 Store in the refrigerator for up to 4 days.

TIP: To cut a fresh pineapple, lay it on its side and slice off the top green leaves and the bottom end. Stand the pineapple upright and carefully slice off the outer skin, removing any eyes that remain. Use your finger or a butter knife to feel where the soft flesh turns tough on the top end of the pineapple and then run a butter knife around this area to mark the core. Use a sharp knife to slice the soft flesh from the core, then discard the core.

Spiced Butternut Squash Soup

The classic fall flavors of cinnamon, nutmeg, and ginger get a blast of heat from crushed red pepper flakes in this creamy, sweet, and spicy soup.

YIELD	SERVING SIZE	PREP TIME	COOK TIME
8 CUPS	**1 CUP**	**10 MINUTES**	**6 TO 8 HOURS**

2½lb (1.25kg) butternut squash, peeled, seeded, and cubed

1 medium yellow onion, diced

1 tsp salt

½ tsp ground cinnamon

¼ tsp ground nutmeg

¼ tsp ground ginger

¼ tsp crushed red pepper flakes

4 cups chicken broth

1 cup heavy cream

1 Add the squash, onion, salt, cinnamon, nutmeg, ginger, red pepper flakes, and chicken broth to a 6- to 8-quart (5.5- to 7.5-liter) slow cooker. Stir to combine.

2 Cover and cook on low for 6 to 8 hours or until the squash is tender.

3 In small batches, carefully transfer the soup to a blender. Fill the blender pitcher no more than half full for each batch, place the lid securely on the pitcher or bowl, and loosen the removable fill cap to create a vent for the steam. Purée in batches for 1 to 2 minutes or until smooth. (Note: Pressure buildup can lead to explosions, so always be sure to vent any steam while puréeing.)

4 Stir in the heavy cream before serving. Store in the refrigerator for up to 4 days.

VARIATION: You can easily substitute other winter squashes in this recipe. Simply replace the butternut squash with a similar-sized pumpkin, acorn squash, or kabocha squash. Each variation will produce a slightly different flavor, but all will work well. Avoid using spaghetti squash; it's far too stringy to work well in a soup.

Russian Red Borscht

This hot beet soup is tangy and sour, and packed with vegetables.
Known for its bold, deep red color, this borscht is just as bold in its flavor.
Caraway and dill provide a familiar, yet exotic, flavor combination.

YIELD	SERVING SIZE	PREP TIME	COOK TIME
12 CUPS	**2 CUPS**	**15 MINUTES**	**6 TO 8 HOURS**

6 medium fresh beets, tops removed, peeled, and diced

2 medium russet potatoes, peeled and diced

1 medium yellow onion, diced

4 medium carrots, peeled and diced

15oz (420g) can kidney beans, drained and rinsed

5 garlic cloves, minced

1 tbsp brown sugar (light or dark), firmly packed

1½ tsp salt

1 tsp dried dill weed

½ tsp caraway seeds

¼ tsp freshly ground black pepper

¼ cup apple cider vinegar

4 cups beef broth

1 bay leaf

4 cups shredded cabbage

Juice of 1 medium lemon

1 Add the beets, potatoes, onion, carrots, kidney beans, and garlic to a 6- to 8-quart (5.5- to 7.5-liter) slow cooker.

2 Sprinkle the brown sugar, salt, dill weed, caraway seeds, and black pepper over the vegetables. Pour in the apple cider vinegar and beef broth, and tuck the bay leaf down into the liquid.

3 Cover and cook on low for 6 to 8 hours. Add the cabbage during the last hour of cooking.

4 Remove the bay leaf and stir in the lemon juice just before serving. (For a smoother borscht, use a blender to purée the soup in batches.) Store in the refrigerator for up to 4 days.

By the Way

Borscht is a classic Eastern European soup known for its deep red color. It's often served topped with a dollop of sour cream and garnished with fresh dill or parsley.

Vegetarian Sweet Potato Chili

Tender sweet potatoes are the star of this bright and flavorful vegetarian chili. Cinnamon complements the sweetness of the sweet potatoes, while cayenne provides some heat to create a perfect balance between sweet and savory.

YIELD	SERVING SIZE	PREP TIME	COOK TIME
12 CUPS	**2 CUPS**	**15 MINUTES**	**6 TO 8 HOURS**

6 medium sweet potatoes, peeled and cubed

1 medium white onion, diced

3 medium celery stalks, sliced

2 large tomatoes, diced

2 garlic cloves, crushed

15oz [420g] can black beans, drained and rinsed

2 tsp paprika

2 tsp ground mustard

1 tsp dried basil

1 tsp salt

¼ tsp ground cinnamon

¼ tsp cayenne

2 cups vegetable broth

1½ tbsp soy sauce

1 bay leaf

1 Add the sweet potatoes, onion, celery, tomatoes, garlic, and black beans to a 6- to 8-quart (5.5- to 7.5-liter) slow cooker.

2 Season with the paprika, mustard, basil, salt, cinnamon, and cayenne. Pour in the vegetable broth and then add the soy sauce. Stir to combine. Tuck the bay leaf down into the liquid.

3 Cover and cook on low for 6 to 8 hours.

4 Remove the bay leaf before serving. Store in the refrigerator for up to 4 days.

By the Way

The terms "sweet potato" and "yam" are often erroneously used synonymously in the United States; they're actually two different kinds of sweet potatoes. Sweet potatoes have a golden skin and a cream-colored flesh, while yams have a copper skin with bright orange flesh. While not a true yam, the latter is often referred to as a yam to distinguish between the two varieties.

White Chicken Chili

In this rich and creamy chili, chicken, white cannellini beans, and green chiles are slowly simmered, thickened with cream cheese, and splashed with heavy cream before serving. Lime juice adds a zip of acidity.

YIELD	SERVING SIZE	PREP TIME	COOK TIME
12 CUPS	**2 CUPS**	**30 MINUTES**	**6 TO 8 HOURS**

2lb (1kg) chicken breasts, trimmed and cut into 1-inch (2.5cm) cubes

2 (15oz [420g]) cans cannellini beans, drained and rinsed

2 (4oz [110g]) cans diced green chiles, with liquid

1 medium yellow onion, diced

1 jalapeño, stemmed, seeded, and minced

4 garlic cloves, minced

1 tbsp ground cumin

1½ tsp salt

1½ tsp ground coriander

1 tsp chili powder

4 cups chicken broth

1 cup heavy whipping cream

8oz (225g) cream cheese, cubed

Juice of 2 medium limes

1 Add the chicken, cannellini beans, green chiles (with liquid), onion, jalapeño, and garlic to a 6- to 8-quart (5.5- to 7.5-liter) slow cooker.

2 Season with the cumin, salt, coriander, and chili powder. Stir to combine and then pour in the chicken broth.

3 Cover and cook on low for 6 to 8 hours.

4 Just before serving, add the heavy whipping cream and cream cheese. Stir until the cream cheese is melted.

5 Stir in the lime juice immediately before serving. Store in the refrigerator for up to 4 days.

By the Way

Achieving a smooth consistency requires that the cheese be cut into cubes and the chili be stirred continuously until the cheese is completely melted. Simply letting the chili sit and then trying to stir in the cheese will result in a lumpy chili. Small pieces and constant movement enable the soft cheese to more easily incorporate with the other liquids.

Texas-Style Beef Chili

Texas would be proud of this no-bean recipe where meaty, tender beef is the star. This chili is perfectly spiced, with a balance of heat and flavor, for a hearty and filling cowboy-style meal.

YIELD	SERVING SIZE	PREP TIME	COOK TIME
12 CUPS	**2 CUPS**	**15 MINUTES**	**8 TO 10 HOURS**

2lb (1kg) beef chuck roast, trimmed and cut into ½-inch (2.5cm) cubes

1 medium yellow onion, diced

2 large red bell peppers, stemmed, ribs and seeds removed, and diced

2 medium celery stalks, sliced

15oz (420g) can diced tomatoes, with juice

4oz (110g) can diced green chiles, with liquid

2 tbsp tomato paste

1 tbsp chili powder

2 tsp cumin

2 tsp paprika

1 tsp onion powder

1 tsp garlic powder

1 tsp salt

1 cup beef broth

2 tbsp Worcestershire sauce

Juice of 1 medium lime

1 Place the chuck roast cubes in a large skillet over high heat. Sear on all sides, about 1 minute per side, then transfer the beef to a 6- to 8-quart (5.5- to 7.5-liter) slow cooker.

2 Add the onion, bell peppers, celery, diced tomatoes (with juice), green chiles (with liquid), and tomato paste.

3 Season with the chili powder, cumin, paprika, onion powder, garlic powder, and salt. Stir to combine. Pour in the beef broth and add the Worcestershire sauce.

4 Cover and cook on low for 8 to 10 hours.

5 Stir in the lime juice before serving. Store in the refrigerator for up to 4 days.

VARIATION: This chili tastes amazing just the way it is, but you can add toppings for even more flavor. Shredded cheddar cheese, sour cream, and chopped fresh cilantro are ideal atop this Texas-style chili.

Winter Leek and Potato Soup

This simple, broth-based version of the classic comfort soup combines the mild sweetness of leeks with the soothing flavors of chicken broth and potatoes. It's a perfect soup to cozy up to on a warm winter evening.

YIELD	SERVING SIZE	PREP TIME	COOK TIME
8 CUPS	**1 CUP**	**10 MINUTES**	**6 TO 8 HOURS**

3 medium leeks

8 medium red potatoes, diced

¼ cup butter

4 cups chicken broth

1 tsp salt

1 Prepare the leeks by trimming off the stringy roots and long green leaves. Slice the white stems lengthwise and rinse out any dirt or debris that might be inside any of the layers. Cut the stems into small slices.

2 Add the leeks, potatoes, and butter to a 6- to 8-quart (5.5- to 7.5-liter) slow cooker. Pour in the chicken broth and then stir in the salt.

3 Cover and cook on low for 6 to 8 hours.

4 Serve chunky, or for a smoother texture, purée in a blender. Fill the blender pitcher no more than half full for each batch. Place the lid securely on the pitcher or bowl and loosen the removable fill cap to create a vent for the steam. Purée until smooth. (Note: Pressure buildup can lead to explosions, so always be sure to vent any steam while puréeing.)

5 Store in the refrigerator for up to 4 days.

VARIATION: For a creamier soup base, add 1 cup heavy whipping cream before serving.

By the Way

Leeks are a member of the onion family and have a mild but distinct flavor. The leek's white stem is the edible part. Leeks can easily hang on to the soil they're grown in, so be sure to clean them well before adding them to your recipe.

Zuppa Toscana (Tuscan Soup)

The time-honored pairing of sausage and potatoes creates a creamy broth for this classic soup. Spicy, hot sausage imparts a kick of both heat and flavor, while kale adds an earthy touch.

YIELD	SERVING SIZE	PREP TIME	COOK TIME
12 CUPS	**2 CUPS**	**10 MINUTES**	**7 TO 9 HOURS**

3 russet potatoes, peeled and cut into 1-inch (2.5cm) chunks

1 medium yellow onion, peeled and diced

4 cups chicken broth

3 garlic cloves, minced

1 tsp salt

1lb (450g) hot sausage, in casings

4 cups chopped kale leaves, loosely packed

1 cup heavy cream

1 Place the potatoes in a 6- to 8-quart (5.5- to 7.5-liter) slow cooker. Add the onion, chicken broth, garlic, and salt. Place the sausage on top of the other ingredients.

2 Cover and cook on low for 6 to 8 hours. During the last hour of cooking, remove the sausage from the slow cooker, slice, and then return it to the slow cooker. Stir in the kale and heavy cream. Cover and continue to cook 1 more hour.

3 Store in the refrigerator for up to 4 days.

VARIATION: If desired, substitute 1 pound (450g) browned and drained ground sausage for the whole sausage.

TIP: Kale is a tougher leafy green that holds up really well in soups, and especially in slow cooking, whereas some other leafy greens like spinach will wilt quickly. If you want to be able to eat this soup right away, use fresh spinach leaves, which will wilt immediately upon being stirred into the soup.

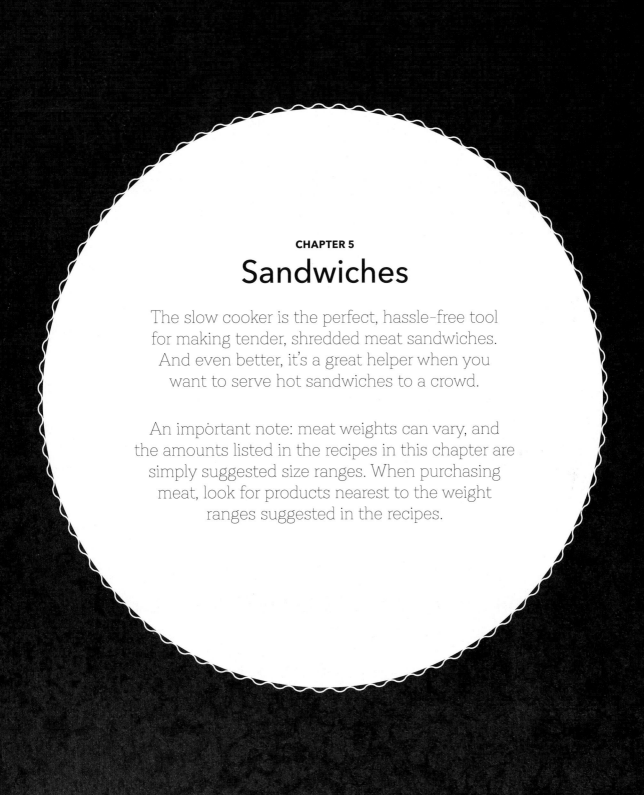

CHAPTER 5

Sandwiches

The slow cooker is the perfect, hassle-free tool
for making tender, shredded meat sandwiches.
And even better, it's a great helper when you
want to serve hot sandwiches to a crowd.

An important note: meat weights can vary, and
the amounts listed in the recipes in this chapter are
simply suggested size ranges. When purchasing
meat, look for products nearest to the weight
ranges suggested in the recipes.

Balsamic Beef Dip Sandwiches

Hot shredded beef roast is simmered in a sweet and tangy *au jus* and served on a French roll to make this the perfect dipping sandwich.

YIELD	SERVING SIZE	PREP TIME	COOK TIME
6 SANDWICHES	**1 SANDWICH**	**5 MINUTES**	**8 TO 10 HOURS**

3- to 4lb (1.5- to 2kg) boneless beef chuck or round roast, cut into ½-inch-thick (1.25cm) strips

1 cup beef broth

½ cup balsamic vinegar

2 tbsp Worcestershire sauce

1 tbsp honey

1 tsp salt

½ tsp garlic powder

½ tsp onion powder

6 French sandwich rolls, sliced

1 Add the beef strips to a 6- to 8-quart (5.5- to 7.5-liter) slow cooker.

2 In a medium bowl, whisk together the beef broth, balsamic vinegar, Worcestershire sauce, honey, salt, garlic powder, and onion powder. Pour the mixture over the meat.

3 Cover and cook on low for 8 to 10 hours.

4 Using two forks, shred the meat in the slow cooker. Strain the meat from the juices, reserving the juices to use as an au jus dip.

5 Serve hot on French rolls with the au jus served on the side for dipping. Store the meat with juices in the refrigerator for up to 4 days.

VARIATION: Peel, halve, and slice 1 medium red onion and place the onion on top of the roast after step 1. Top the sandwiches with the cooked onions and sliced pepperoncinis.

By the Way

Au jus is a French term meaning "with juice." The jus in this recipe comes from the natural juices of the meat and is enhanced by the added seasonings. You can serve the sandwich without the jus, but the dipping jus really enhances the flavor of the sandwich.

Barbecue Pulled Pork Sandwiches

In this mouthwatering sandwich, pork roast is simmered in a homemade barbeque sauce to produce tender, pull-apart meat that's infused with dark, sweet barbecue flavors.

YIELD	SERVING SIZE	PREP TIME	COOK TIME
8 SANDWICHES	**1 SANDWICH**	**5 MINUTES**	**8 TO 10 HOURS**

3- to 4lb (1.5- to 2kg) boneless pork butt or shoulder roast, cut into ½-inch (1.25cm) pieces

1 medium yellow onion, halved and sliced

1 cup ketchup

¼ cup brown sugar (light or dark), firmly packed

¼ cup Worcestershire sauce

2 tbsp red wine vinegar

2 tsp garlic powder

½ tsp salt

½ tsp crushed red pepper flakes

½ tsp ground mustard

8 hamburger buns

1 Add the pork pieces to a 6- to 8-quart (5.5- to 7.5-liter) slow cooker. Top with the onion slices.

2 In a small bowl, combine the ketchup, brown sugar, Worcestershire sauce, red wine vinegar, garlic powder, salt, crushed red pepper flakes, and mustard. Stir until well combined and then pour the sauce over the pork.

3 Cover and cook on low for 8 to 10 hours.

4 Using two forks, shred the meat. Spoon ¾ to 1 cup of the meat onto each bun and serve hot. Store the filling in the refrigerator for up to 4 days.

VARIATION: Add 2 teaspoons liquid smoke to the sauce to add a nice, smoky flavor.

TIP: If you want to use bottled barbecue sauce instead of making your own, you'll need to change the recipe slightly to avoid burning the sauce. Proceed with step 1 as directed then, instead of following step 2, just add 2 cups of water to the slow cooker. Cover and cook on low for 8 to 10 hours and then drain any excess liquid from the slow cooker. Shred the pork as directed in step 4, and then add 2 cups bottled barbecue sauce. Toss the meat in the sauce and serve immediately or let the meat and sauce heat through on low for 1 additional hour.

Extra-Sloppy Joes

Sloppy joes get a slow cooker makeover in this recipe. The low, slow cooking deepens the flavors, giving you a sandwich bursting with flavor. One warning: these can get messy, so napkins are required!

YIELD	SERVING SIZE	PREP TIME	COOK TIME
8 SANDWICHES	**1 SANDWICH**	**10 MINUTES**	**4 TO 6 HOURS**

1lb (450g) lean ground beef

1 medium yellow onion, halved and sliced

1 large green bell pepper, stemmed, ribs and seeds removed, and diced

2 medium celery stalks, diced

2 medium carrots, peeled and diced

8oz (225g) can tomato sauce

6oz (170g) can tomato paste

2 tbsp Worcestershire sauce

4 garlic cloves, peeled and minced

1 tbsp brown sugar (light or dark), firmly packed

1 tsp salt

1 tsp ground mustard

½ tsp crushed red pepper flakes

8 hamburger buns

1 Add the ground beef and onions to a large skillet over medium-high heat. Sauté for about 5 minutes, stirring occasionally, until the beef is browned. Drain any excess fat from the skillet.

2 Transfer the beef and onions to a 6- to 8-quart (5.5- to 7.5-liter) slow cooker.

3 Add the bell pepper, celery, carrots, tomato sauce, tomato paste, Worcestershire sauce, garlic, brown sugar, salt, mustard, and crushed red pepper flakes. Stir to combine.

4 Cover and cook on low for 4 to 6 hours.

5 Spoon about ½ to ¾ cup of the meat mixture onto each bun and serve hot. Store the meat mixture in the refrigerator for up to 4 days.

VARIATION: For a lighter version, substitute 1 pound (450g) ground turkey for the ground beef.

TIP: Before adding ground meats to a slow cooker, you should first brown them in a skillet to remove any excess fat. You don't have to completely cook the meat because it will cook thoroughly in the slow cooker, you simply need to brown it to the point that the excess fats are released so you can then drain them off.

Greek Chicken Gyros

Zippy chicken breast is topped with lemon juice and garlic, and served in a pita flatbread with tangy cucumber yogurt tzatziki sauce in this slow-cooked version of the classic Greek sandwich.

YIELD	SERVING SIZE	PREP TIME	COOK TIME
6 SANDWICHES	**1 SANDWICH**	**10 MINUTES**	**4 TO 6 HOURS**

1 medium red onion, halved and thinly sliced, divided

2lb (1kg) boneless, skinless chicken breasts, trimmed

¼ cup red wine vinegar

Juice of 1 medium lemon

1 tbsp olive oil

6 garlic cloves, minced

½ tsp dried oregano

½ tsp dried basil

⅛ tsp freshly ground black pepper

Zest of 1 medium lemon

1 cup plain Greek yogurt

2 tbsp minced fresh dill

¼ tsp salt

1 medium cucumber, peeled

6 pita or Arabic flatbreads

3 cups romaine lettuce, chopped

2 Roma tomatoes, sliced

1 Layer half of the onions in the bottom of a 6- to 8-quart (5.5- to 7.5-liter) slow cooker. Place the chicken breasts on top of the onions.

2 Pour the red wine vinegar and lemon juice over the chicken. Drizzle with the olive oil.

3 Sprinkle the garlic over the chicken, followed by the oregano, basil, black pepper, and lemon zest.

4 Cover and cook on low for 4 to 6 hours.

5 While the chicken is cooking, add the Greek yogurt, dill, and salt to a medium bowl. Stir to combine.

6 Cut the cucumber in half. Finely dice half of the cucumber and thinly slice the remaining half. Set aside the sliced cucumbers. Stir the diced cucumbers into the yogurt mixture and transfer to the refrigerator until ready to serve.

7 To serve, spoon ½ cup of the chicken onto half of each pita, and top with ½ cup romaine lettuce, a few red onion slices, 4 to 6 cucumber slices, 3 to 5 Roma tomato slices, and 1 heaping spoonful of the yogurt tzatziki sauce. Fold over the pita and serve. Store in the refrigerator for up to 4 days.

VARIATION: For a wide variety of flavors, you can use other sauces and even salad dressings like ranch, honey mustard, Italian, or blue cheese in place of the tzatziki sauce.

Philly Cheesesteak Sandwiches

Thin-sliced steak is smothered with seasoned bell peppers, onions, and provolone cheese, making this sandwich as mouthwatering as it is messy.

YIELD	SERVING SIZE	PREP TIME	COOK TIME
6 SANDWICHES	**1 SANDWICH**	**5 MINUTES**	**6 TO 8 HOURS**

2lb (1kg) round steak, ½-inch (1.25cm) slices

4 large bell peppers (any color), ribs and seeds removed, and sliced

1 medium red onion, halved and sliced

2 tsp sugar

1 tsp salt

1 tsp garlic powder

½ tsp dried oregano

½ tsp dried basil

½ tsp freshly ground black pepper

6 hoagie rolls, sliced

6 slices provolone cheese

1 Add the round steak, bell peppers, and onion slices to a 6- to 8-quart (5.5- to 7.5-liter) slow cooker.

2 Season the meat and vegetables with the sugar, salt, garlic powder, oregano, basil, and black pepper. Stir to combine.

3 Cover and cook on low for 6 to 8 hours.

4 Preheat the broiler.

5 Strain any excess liquids from the slow cooker. Spoon about 1 cup of the meat mixture into each hoagie roll.

6 Top each sandwich with 1 slice of provolone cheese.

7 Place the sandwiches on a baking sheet and broil for 2 to 3 minutes or until the cheese is melted and bubbly.

8 Serve hot. Store the meat mixture in the refrigerator for up to 4 days.

VARIATION: Add 1 pound (450g) sliced button mushrooms when you add the bell peppers and onion slices in step 1.

By the Way

Toasting the bread helps keep it from getting overly soggy from the meat and accompanying liquids.

Spicy Italian Chicken Sandwiches

Spicy chicken is covered with melted cheese and heaps of slow-roasted red peppers in this delicious Italian sandwich served on focaccia.

YIELD	SERVING SIZE	PREP TIME	COOK TIME
6 SANDWICHES	**1 SANDWICH**	**5 MINUTES**	**4 TO 6 HOURS**

2lb (1kg) boneless, skinless chicken breasts, trimmed

2 tbsp olive oil

½ tsp salt

½ tsp garlic powder

½ tsp dried basil

¼ tsp dried oregano

¼ tsp crushed red pepper flakes

⅛ tsp freshly ground black pepper

2 large red bell peppers, ribs and seeds removed, and sliced

2 cups shredded mozzarella cheese

2 (1lb [450g]) loaves focaccia

2 cups fresh spinach leaves

1 Add the chicken breasts to a 6- to 8-quart (5.5- to 7.5-liter) slow cooker.

2 Drizzle the olive oil over the chicken and then season with the salt, garlic powder, basil, oregano, red pepper flakes, and black pepper.

3 Arrange the bell pepper slices over the chicken.

4 Cover and cook on low for 4 to 6 hours.

5 Using a fork, pull apart the chicken into large chunks or use a knife to cut into slices. Top immediately with the mozzarella cheese and allow the cheese to melt.

6 Cut each focaccia loaf into 3 pieces and then split each piece horizontally to create tops and bottoms for 6 sandwiches.

7 Spoon ½ cup of the chicken, peppers, and cheese onto each sandwich. Top with ⅓ cup spinach leaves and serve. Store the filling in the refrigerator for up to 4 days.

VARIATION: These sandwiches are great served with a quick and easy garlic aioli. To make the aioli, combine ½ cup mayonnaise with 3 cloves crushed garlic, 1 tablespoon lemon juice, and ½ teaspoon salt in a small bowl.

Vietnamese Pulled Pork Banh Mi

Tender Vietnamese shredded pork with pickled vegetables, hot jalapeño slices, and fresh cilantro served on a crusty French baguette makes for a sensational variation of this trendy Vietnamese sandwich.

YIELD	SERVING SIZE	PREP TIME	COOK TIME
6 SANDWICHES	**1 SANDWICH**	**10 MINUTES**	**8 TO 10 HOURS**

2- to 3lb (1- to 1.5kg) boneless pork butt or shoulder roast

1 cup chicken broth

¼ cup soy sauce

2 tbsp fish sauce

½ tsp ground ginger

3 garlic cloves, peeled and minced

1 medium daikon radish, julienned or shredded

2 large carrots, julienned or shredded

¼ cup rice vinegar

Juice of 1 medium lime

6 crusty baguettes, sliced

1 medium cucumber, sliced

3 cups fresh cilantro leaves

1 jalapeño, thinly sliced

1 Add the pork butt roast to a 6- to 8-quart (5.5- to 7.5-liter) slow cooker.

2 Pour in the chicken broth, soy sauce, and fish sauce, and then stir in the ginger and garlic.

3 Cover and cook on low for 8 to 10 hours.

4 Meanwhile, in a small bowl, combine the daikon radish and carrots. Top with the rice vinegar. Cover and refrigerate until ready to serve.

5 Just before serving, use two forks to shred the pork and then stir in the lime juice.

6 Spoon ½ cup of the meat, hot or cold, onto each crusty baguette. Top with the daikon radish and carrot mixture, cucumber slices, cilantro leaves, and jalapeño slices. Serve promptly. Store the filling in the refrigerator for up to 4 days.

By the Way

Fish sauce can be an intimidating ingredient if you've never worked with it. It's one of those unusual ingredients that has an unpleasant aroma, but it adds a real depth of flavor to a dish. You can omit the fish sauce in this recipe if you like, but the flavor of the meat might fall slightly flat as a result. The fish sauce helps develop those rich and tangy flavors of southeast Asia.

CHAPTER 6
Beef and Lamb

The slow cooker is the ideal braising tool for turning tough cuts of red meat that require long, slow cooking methods into melt-in-your-mouth finished meals. In this chapter, you'll discover several takes on some American beef and lamb classics, as well as some flavorful red meat recipes with a more global flair.

Note that due to the nature of red meat, the recipes in this chapter that utilize tougher cuts are cooked on the low setting because they need a long, slow, and low cooking process to tenderize.

Korean Beef Bulgogi

Flavorful, spicy beef melts in your mouth in this slow-cooked Korean classic. Sweet and spicy, this barbecue-style beef dish will please any palate.

YIELD	SERVING SIZE	PREP TIME	COOK TIME
2 POUNDS (1KG)	**⅓ POUND (150G)**	**5 MINUTES**	**6 TO 8 HOURS**

2lb (1kg) flank steak, cut against the grain into ¼-inch (10cm) strips

⅓ cup soy sauce

¼ cup brown sugar (light or dark), firmly packed

2 tbsp sesame seeds

1 tbsp sesame oil

3 garlic cloves, peeled and minced

½ tsp crushed red pepper flakes

½ tsp ground ginger

2 tsp oyster sauce

½ cup sliced green onions (green parts only)

1 Add the steak strips to a 6- to 8-quart (5.5- to 7.5-liter) slow cooker.

2 In a small bowl, combine the soy sauce, brown sugar, sesame seeds, sesame oil, garlic, red pepper flakes, ginger, and oyster sauce. Whisk to combine and then pour the mixture over the steak strips.

3 Cover and cook on low for 6 to 8 hours.

4 Garnish with green onions and serve alone or over rice. Store in the refrigerator for up to 4 days.

By the Way

Cutting against the grain is important when working with beef—think of the grain as the natural breaking point of the meat. Cutting against the grain yields the maximum number of breaking points in each bite, ensuring every bite almost falls apart in your mouth. The flank steak used in this recipe has a highly visible grain and looks almost striped.

Braised Beef Short Ribs

Slow-braised beef short ribs fall right off the bone for a tender, succulent beef dish that warms you from the inside out.

YIELD	SERVING SIZE	PREP TIME	COOK TIME
8 RIBS	**1 RIB**	**5 MINUTES**	**8 HOURS**

1 tbsp olive oil

8 beef short ribs

2 cups beef broth

¼ cup Worcestershire sauce

1 tsp onion powder

1 tsp garlic powder

1 tsp salt

½ tsp freshly ground black pepper

1 In a large skillet over high heat, heat the olive oil. Add the short ribs and sear for about 30 seconds per side or until all the exposed meat is browned. Remove from the heat.

2 Combine the beef broth, Worcestershire sauce, onion powder, and garlic powder in a 6- to 8-quart (5.5- to 7.5-liter) slow cooker.

3 Season the short ribs with the salt and black pepper and then place the ribs in the slow cooker.

4 Cover and cook on low for 8 hours.

5 Serve hot. Store in the refrigerator for up to 4 days.

VARIATION: For an extra layer of flavor, replace 1 cup beef broth with 1 cup red wine.

TIP: You can buy short ribs boneless or bone-in. Both can be used in this recipe with the same cooking time.

By the Way

Braising is typically reserved for tough cuts of meat. Traditional braising involves searing meat at a high heat and then finishing in a pot with a liquid. A slow cooker is the perfect braising tool because it can braise with very low heat, allowing the tough collagen and fibers in the meat to slowly melt away.

Honey Garlic Barbecue Beef Ribs

These hearty beef ribs are slow roasted and completed with a homemade, hickory-smoked, honey garlic barbecue sauce.

YIELD	SERVING SIZE	PREP TIME	COOK TIME
8 RIBS	**1 RIB**	**5 MINUTES**	**8 TO 10 HOURS**

8 whole beef ribs

2 cups ketchup

12 garlic cloves, minced

2 tbsp hot sauce

¼ cup honey

2 tbsp molasses

2 tbsp brown sugar
(light or dark)

1 tbsp hickory flavor
liquid smoke

1 tbsp cornstarch

1 tsp Worcestershire sauce

1 tsp soy sauce

1 tsp salt

1 tsp onion powder

1 tsp garlic powder

1 tsp dried oregano

1 tsp dried basil

½ tsp freshly ground
black pepper

¼ tsp cayenne

¼ tsp paprika

1 Add the ribs to a 6- to 8-quart (5.5- to 7.5-liter) slow cooker. (Cut the ribs to fit, if necessary, and then stack.)

2 In a medium bowl, combine the ketchup, garlic, hot sauce, honey, molasses, brown sugar, liquid smoke, cornstarch, Worcestershire sauce, soy sauce, salt, onion powder, garlic powder, oregano, basil, black pepper, cayenne, and paprika.

3 Pour the sauce over the ribs, making sure all the ribs are coated with the sauce.

4 Cover and cook on low for 8 to 10 hours.

5 Serve hot. Store in the refrigerator for up to 4 days.

TIP: Cooking on high is not recommended for this cut.

By the Way

Ribs have a tough membrane on the bottom or back side that can create a chewy bite. You can remove it easily before cooking by turning the ribs face down and rubbing your fingers along the edge of a rib to release the membrane. It will easily loosen, and you can then pull the strip off the ribs.

Modern Meatloaf

This modern twist on the classic ground beef loaf, complete with a spicy glaze, has a nice level of heat for a full-flavored meatloaf.

YIELD	SERVING SIZE	PREP TIME	COOK TIME
8 SLICES	**1 SLICE**	**10 MINUTES**	**4 TO 5 HOURS**

1lb (450g) lean ground beef

½ medium yellow onion, diced

1 cup breadcrumbs

½ cup reduced fat (2%) milk

3 tbsp Worcestershire sauce, divided

1 tsp salt

1 tsp dried basil

1 tsp dried oregano

½ tsp freshly ground black pepper

½ tsp crushed red pepper flakes

½ cup ketchup

2 tbsp brown sugar (light or dark)

2 tsp hot sauce

1 In a large bowl, combine the ground beef, onion, breadcrumbs, milk, 2 tablespoons Worcestershire sauce, salt, basil, oregano, black pepper, and red pepper flakes.

2 Using your hands, knead the ingredients for about 1 minute or until well combined. Form the mixture into a loaf shape and place it in a 6- to 8-quart (5.5- to 7.5-liter) slow cooker.

3 In a small bowl, combine the ketchup, brown sugar, remaining 1 tablespoon Worcestershire sauce, and hot sauce. Pour the sauce over the meatloaf.

4 Cover and cook on high 4 to 5 hours.

5 Slice and serve hot. Store in the refrigerator for up to 4 days.

VARIATION: For a nutrient boost, use any combination of ground flaxseed, wheat germ, and wheat bran to replace the 1 cup breadcrumbs.

By the Way

Using a lean ground beef is important for a slow-cooked meatloaf because the fat in the beef has nowhere to drain in the slow cooker. Ground sirloin works particularly well because it has a low 8 to 10 percent fat content.

Midwestern Beef Brisket

Smoky brisket rubbed with flavorful spices makes for a hearty meal you'd never guess came from a humble slow cooker.

YIELD	SERVING SIZE	PREP TIME	COOK TIME
3 POUNDS (1.5KG)	**⅓ POUND (150G)**	**5 MINUTES**	**6 TO 8 HOURS**

3- to 4lb (1.5- to 2kg) beef brisket

4 tbsp liquid smoke

¼ cup Worcestershire sauce

1 tsp salt

1 tsp garlic powder

½ tsp chili powder

½ tsp paprika

½ tsp onion powder

½ tsp freshly ground black pepper

½ tsp cayenne

1 medium yellow onion, diced

1 Add the brisket to a 6- to 8-quart (5.5- to 7.5-liter) slow cooker.

2 Pour the liquid smoke and Worcestershire sauce over the brisket.

3 In a small bowl, combine the salt, garlic powder, chili powder, paprika, onion powder, black pepper, and cayenne. Rub the spice mixture over the top of the brisket. Top with the onion.

4 Cover and cook on low for 6 to 8 hours.

5 Serve hot. Store in the refrigerator for up to 4 days.

VARIATION: For **Jewish-Style Brisket,** use 1 cup red wine in place of the liquid smoke, and instead of the seasoning mixture called for in step 3, rub the brisket with a combination of 1 teaspoon salt, 1 teaspoon garlic powder, 1 teaspoon dried rosemary, 1 teaspoon dried oregano, ½ teaspoon black pepper, and ½ teaspoon dried basil.

By the Way

Brisket is perhaps one of the toughest cuts of beef because it comes from the cow's pectoral muscles, which support the majority of the cow's weight. The tough connective tissue needs long, slow cooking in order to yield a tender result, so cooking on high is not recommended for this cut.

Leg of Lamb with Rosemary, Lemon, and Garlic

Tender, slow-roasted leg of lamb is classically paired with the flavors of rosemary, lemon, and garlic for this simple, slow-cooked version of an elegant meal.

YIELD	SERVING SIZE	PREP TIME	COOK TIME
3 TO 4 POUNDS (1.5 TO 2KG)	**⅓ POUND (150G)**	**5 MINUTES**	**8 TO 10 HOURS**

4- to 6lb (2- to 2.75kg) bone-in leg of lamb

Juice of 2 medium lemons

10 garlic cloves, minced

1 tbsp dried rosemary

2 tsp salt

1 tsp freshly ground black pepper

1 large yellow onion, diced

1 Add the leg of lamb to a 6- to 8-quart (5.5- to 7.5-liter) slow cooker.

2 Pour the lemon juice over the lamb. Rub the lamb with the garlic, rosemary, salt, and black pepper.

3 Sprinkle the onion over the top of the lamb.

4 Cover and cook on low for 8 to 10 hours.

5 Serve hot. Store in the refrigerator for up to 4 days.

VARIATION: For a richer flavor, pour ½ cup red wine over the lamb along with the lemon juice.

TIP: Cooking on high is not recommended for this cut.

By the Way

Leg of lamb is sold in both bone-in and boneless versions, and either will work well in this recipe. Boneless leg of lamb is often sold with a netting around it to help hold its shape while cooking. You can leave this netting in place because it's designed to withstand the cooking. However, do remove it before serving.

Sunday Afternoon Pot Roast

This seasoned chuck roast is slowly simmered and surrounded by carrots and onions for a fall-apart-tender beef dish. It's the perfect comfort meal for a Sunday afternoon family dinner.

YIELD	SERVING SIZE	PREP TIME	COOK TIME
2 POUNDS (1KG)	**¼ POUND (110G)**	**10 MINUTES**	**6 TO 8 HOURS**

2- to 3lb (1- to 1.5kg) chuck roast

½ tsp salt

¼ tsp freshly ground black pepper

1 medium yellow onion, cut into large chunks

1lb (450g) carrots, peeled and cut into 2-inch (5cm) pieces

1 cup beef broth

2 tbsp Worcestershire sauce

3 garlic cloves, minced

1 Add the chuck roast to a 6- to 8-quart (5.5- to 7.5-liter) slow cooker.

2 Season with the salt and black pepper. Place the onion on top of the roast and surround the roast with the carrots.

3 Pour the beef broth and Worcestershire sauce over the carrots. Sprinkle the garlic over the roast and vegetables.

4 Cover and cook on low for 6 to 8 hours.

5 Use two forks to shred the roast before serving. Store in the refrigerator for up to 4 days.

VARIATION: For a hearty one-pot meal, add 6 medium red potatoes, cut into bite-sized chunks, and 4 medium stalks celery, sliced. Place the vegetables on the bottom of the slow cooker and the meat on top.

TIP: Cooking on high is not recommended for this cut.

> ## By the Way
>
> Pot roasts utilize large, tough cuts of beef, particularly the chuck. The fibrous meat slowly breaks down as it braises in the slow cooker, turning that tough, chewy meat into a tender and flavorful bite.

Triple Citrus Lamb Shanks

Tender lamb shank is slowly braised in tangy citrus juices of orange, lemon, and lime. The vegetable-based braising liquid is tart and flavorful, and provides a saucy addition to the succulent lamb.

YIELD	SERVING SIZE	PREP TIME	COOK TIME
6 SHANKS	**1 SHANK**	**15 MINUTES**	**8 HOURS**

2 tbsp olive oil

6 whole lamb shanks

2 medium carrots, peeled and finely diced

2 medium celery stalks, finely diced

1 large sweet onion, minced

3 garlic cloves, minced

2 tbsp tomato paste

1 cup chicken broth

1 tsp salt

Zest and juice of 1 medium orange

Zest and juice of 1 medium lemon

Zest and juice of 1 medium lime

1 In a large skillet over high heat, heat the olive oil. Add the lamb shanks and sear on all sides, about 5 to 7 minutes.

2 In a medium bowl, combine the carrots, celery, onion, garlic, tomato paste, chicken broth, salt, orange zest, orange juice, lemon zest, lemon juice, lime zest, and lime juice.

3 Transfer the seared lamb shanks to a 6- to 8-quart (5.5- to 7.5-liter) slow cooker and pour the vegetable mixture over the lamb shanks.

4 Cover and cook on low for 8 hours.

5 Strain the vegetables from the braising liquid and use as a topping for lamb. Serve hot.

VARIATION: For a punch of flavor, add ½ cup red wine to the braising liquid.

TIP: Cooking on high is not recommended for this cut.

By the Way

A shank often weighs upward of 1 pound (450g), which can make for quite a large serving size. If you feel the shank is too large, use a fork to shred the meat from the bone and then serve it in a large bowl with the strained vegetables and a little braising liquid.

CHAPTER 7

Chicken

Chicken is the perfect protein for the slow cooker! It's incredibly easy to prepare, and because it's a lean meat, you can cook it on the high setting.

Note that the recipes in this chapter are intended for use in 6- to 8-quart (5.5- to 7.5-liter) slow cookers. Smaller 6-quart models will use the shorter cooking times, while larger 8-quart models likely will require the entire range of time listed. Also note that bone-in chicken will take longer to cook than boneless chicken. All the recipes in this chapter, with the exception of the Herb-Roasted Whole Chicken, can be doubled in a larger slow cooker.

Herb-Roasted Whole Chicken

This delicious whole chicken is made from start to finish in the slow cooker; it's a rotisserie-like chicken you can simply prep and forget. Crusted with herbs and moistened by butter, this chicken is moist and tender.

YIELD	SERVING SIZE	PREP TIME	COOK TIME
2 TO 3 POUNDS (1 TO 1.5KG)	**⅓ POUND (150G)**	**10 MINUTES**	**5 TO 8 HOURS**

3- to 5lb (1.5- to 2.5kg) whole chicken

¼ cup butter

3 medium lemons

1 tsp dried rosemary

1 tsp dried oregano

1 tsp dried basil

1 tsp salt

½ tsp freshly ground black pepper

1 Create a platform for the chicken by crumpling four large pieces of aluminum foil into balls and placing them in the bottom of a 6- to 8-quart (5.5- to 7.5-liter) slow cooker. (This will help prevent the skin on the underside of the chicken from melting.)

2 Remove and discard the giblets and neck parts (if any) from the cavity of the chicken.

3 Using your finger, loosen the skin on the chicken by sliding it in at both ends. Divide the butter into small pieces and insert the pieces in between the skin and meat of the chicken.

4 Place the chicken in the slow cooker, breast side down.

5 Cut the lemons in half and squeeze the juice over the chicken, and then stuff the squeezed lemon rinds into the chicken cavity.

6 Sprinkle the rosemary, oregano, basil, salt, and black pepper over the chicken.

7 Cover and cook on low for 8 hours or on high for 5 to 6 hours.

8 Remove and discard the lemon rinds. Serve the chicken hot. Store in the refrigerator for up to 4 days.

VARIATION: For **Cajun Chicken,** replace the rosemary, oregano, and basil with 1 tablespoon Cajun seasoning spice mix.

Chicken Tikka Masala

Tender chunks of chicken are simmered in a spicy, tomato-based sauce and flavored with garam masala. Heavy cream gives the sensational sauce an added richness.

YIELD	SERVING SIZE	PREP TIME	COOK TIME
6 CUPS	**1 CUP**	**5 MINUTES**	**4 TO 8 HOURS**

2lb (1kg) boneless, skinless chicken breasts, trimmed and cut into 1-inch (2.5cm) cubes

3 garlic cloves, minced

1 jalapeño, stemmed and minced

1 tbsp paprika

2 tsp cumin

2 tsp garam masala

2 (8oz [225g]) cans tomato sauce

2 tbsp tomato paste

1½ tsp salt

1 cup heavy whipping cream

½ cup chopped fresh cilantro

1 Add the chicken breasts to a 6- to 8-quart (5.5- to 7.5-liter) slow cooker.

2 Stir in the garlic, jalapeño, paprika, cumin, garam masala, tomato sauce, tomato paste, and salt.

3 Cover and cook on low for 6 to 8 hours or on high for 4 to 5 hours.

4 When ready to serve, stir in the heavy whipping cream and garnish with the cilantro. Store in the refrigerator for up to 4 days.

VARIATION: You can use this same sauce mixture over lamb or the Indian cheese *paneer*, or make a vegetable version using cauliflower.

By the Way

Tikka is a word used in Indian and Pakistani cuisine to denote chunks of meat in a spice marinade. *Garam masala* is an Indian spice mixture of cumin, coriander, cardamom, black pepper, cinnamon, cloves, and nutmeg. The whole spices are toasted and ground into a distinctly flavorful mixture. Garam masala is sold in the spice section of most grocery stores.

Coconut Chicken Curry

Bite-sized pieces of chicken are gently stewed in this sweet curry. The flavors of coconut and acidic tomatoes bring out the bright notes of the sauce.

YIELD	SERVING SIZE	PREP TIME	COOK TIME
6 CUPS	**1 CUP**	**5 MINUTES**	**4 TO 8 HOURS**

2lb (1kg) boneless, skinless chicken breasts, trimmed and cut into 1-inch (2.5cm) cubes

½ large sweet onion, diced

4 garlic cloves, minced

14oz (400g) can coconut milk

15oz (420g) can diced tomatoes, drained

8oz (225g) can tomato sauce

2 tbsp curry powder

1 tbsp sugar

1 tsp salt

1 Add the chicken breasts, onion, and garlic to a 6- to 8-quart (5.5- to 7.5-liter) slow cooker.

2 Pour in the coconut milk, diced tomatoes, and tomato sauce. Stir in the curry powder, sugar, and salt.

3 Cover and cook on low for 6 to 8 hours or on high for 4 to 5 hours.

4 Serve hot. Store in the refrigerator for up to 4 days.

VARIATION: To increase the spiciness, add 1 teaspoon crushed red pepper flakes.

By the Way

Curry powder is a spice mixture with no set ingredients or proportions, so every curry powder is different. Many curry blends found in the United States and other Western countries commonly contain coriander, fenugreek, red pepper, and turmeric. (Turmeric is the ingredient that gives curry powder its yellow color.) Experiment with different brands of curry powder to find one to your liking.

Chicken Cacciatore

Chicken breast is slow braised in a simmering sauce of tomatoes, onion, bell pepper, and herbs. The chicken is dredged and browned prior to slow cooking for an added depth of texture and flavor.

YIELD	SERVING SIZE	PREP TIME	COOK TIME
3 CHICKEN BREASTS	**½ CHICKEN BREAST**	**10 MINUTES**	**4 TO 8 HOURS**

1 cup all-purpose flour

1½ tsp salt, divided

1½ tsp dried basil, divided

1 tsp paprika

1 tsp freshly ground black pepper, divided

3 (½- to ¾lb [225- to 340g]) boneless, skinless chicken breasts, trimmed

2 tbsp olive oil

1 medium yellow onion, diced

2 garlic cloves, minced

1 large green bell pepper, ribs and seeds removed, and diced

15oz (420g) can diced tomatoes, with juice

½ tsp dried oregano

1 In a shallow bowl, stir together the all-purpose flour, 1 teaspoon salt, 1 teaspoon basil, paprika, and ½ teaspoon black pepper.

2 Place the chicken breasts in the flour mixture and turn to coat each side.

3 In a large skillet over medium-high heat, heat the olive oil. Add the chicken and sear for 3 minutes per side. Transfer the chicken breasts to a 6- to 8-quart (5.5- to 7.5-liter) slow cooker.

4 Add the onion, garlic, bell pepper, tomatoes (with juice), remaining ½ teaspoon salt, remaining ½ teaspoon basil, remaining ½ teaspoon black pepper, and oregano to the slow cooker.

5 Cover and cook on high for 4 to 5 hours or on low for 6 to 8 hours.

6 Serve hot, topped with the sauce. Store in the refrigerator for up to 4 days.

VARIATION: When ready to serve, heat a large skillet over high heat. Add 1 tablespoon olive oil and 8 ounces (225g) sliced button mushrooms. Cook, stirring occasionally, for 5 minutes. Serve the mushrooms over the top of the hot chicken.

Green Chile Chicken Enchilada Casserole

Layers of creamy green chile chicken and flour tortillas are slow-cooked casserole-style. This "enchilada" dinner is rich and decadent.

YIELD	SERVING SIZE	PREP TIME	COOK TIME
8 SLICES	**1 SLICE**	**15 MINUTES**	**4 TO 8 HOURS**

4 tbsp butter

2 garlic cloves, minced

⅓ cup all-purpose flour

1 tsp chili powder

1 tsp cumin

1 tsp salt

2 cups chicken broth

4 cups cooked and shredded chicken

1 medium yellow onion, diced

1 cup sour cream

2 (4oz [110g]) cans diced green chiles, with liquid

10 (7.5-inch [20cm]) flour tortillas

2 cups shredded Monterey Jack cheese

1 In a medium saucepan over low heat, melt the butter. Increase the heat to medium and add the garlic. Cook for 1 more minute.

2 Whisk in the flour, chili powder, cumin, and salt to form a paste. Pour in the chicken broth, increase the heat to high, and whisk until the sauce reaches a simmer and thickens, then remove from the heat and transfer to a large bowl, reserving about ¼ cup of the sauce.

3 Add the shredded chicken, onion, sour cream, and green chiles (with liquid) to the remaining sauce. Stir to combine.

4 Place 2 tortillas in the bottom of a 6- to 8-quart (5.5- to 7.5-liter) oval slow cooker, overlapping them in the middle. (If you're using a round slow cooker, only use 1 tortilla in each layer.)

5 Top the tortilla(s) with ¼ of the chicken mixture and then top with ¼ cup Monterey Jack cheese. Repeat layering with 4 chicken layers. Top the last layer with the final layer of tortilla(s) and then spread just enough of the reserved sauce over the top to wet the tortillas. Top with the remaining 1 cup of cheese.

6 Cover and cook on low for 6 to 8 hours or on high for 4 to 5 hours.

7 Cut into 8 slices and serve hot as is, or topped with a dollop of sour cream and chopped fresh cilantro, if desired. Store in the refrigerator for up to 4 days.

Honey Chipotle Barbecue Chicken Drumsticks

Tender drumsticks are simmered in a honey chipotle barbecue sauce. The chipotle brings both heat and smokiness to the homemade sauce.

YIELD	SERVING SIZE	PREP TIME	COOK TIME
12 DRUMSTICKS	**2 DRUMSTICKS**	**5 MINUTES**	**4 TO 8 HOURS**

12 chicken drumsticks

½ cup ketchup

¼ cup brown sugar (light or dark), firmly packed

¼ cup honey

1 chipotle chile in adobo sauce, finely chopped

2 tsp apple cider vinegar

1½ tsp Worcestershire sauce

½ tsp garlic powder

¼ tsp salt

1 pinch freshly ground black pepper

1 Add the drumsticks to a 6- to 8-quart (5.5- to 7.5-liter) slow cooker.

2 In a small bowl, whisk together the ketchup, brown sugar, honey, chipotle chile and adobo sauce, apple cider vinegar, Worcestershire sauce, garlic powder, salt, and black pepper. Pour the barbecue sauce over the chicken.

3 Cover and cook on low for 6 to 8 hours or on high for 4 to 5 hours.

4 Serve hot. Store in the refrigerator for up to 4 days.

TIP: You can use any bone-in chicken parts in place of the drumsticks. Thighs, wings, and bone-in chicken breasts are all suitable. Wings require the lower range of cooking time because they're small, while bone-in breasts require the maximum cooking time due to their larger size.

By the Way

Chipotle chiles in adobo sauce are canned, smoked jalapeños. They have a distinct smoky flavor and are spicy, so recipes often call for only a small amount. To increase the heat, you can add more chipotle chiles to this recipe, but be sure to taste as you add them to be sure it doesn't get too hot.

Orange Chicken

A sweet orange sauce envelopes bite-sized pieces of chicken for a slow-cooked version of the popular restaurant dish.

YIELD	SERVING SIZE	PREP TIME	COOK TIME
3 CUPS	**½ CUP**	**5 MINUTES**	**4 TO 8 HOURS**

2lb (1kg) boneless, skinless chicken breasts, trimmed and cut into bite-sized pieces

1 medium orange

⅓ cup brown sugar (light or dark), firmly packed

1 tsp cornstarch

1 tsp ground ginger

1 tsp crushed red pepper flakes

1 cup orange juice

¼ cup rice vinegar

2 tbsp soy sauce

1 Add the chicken pieces to a 6- to 8-quart (5.5- to 7.5-liter) slow cooker.

2 Using a zester or a small grater, zest the orange. (You'll need about 1 to 2 tablespoons zest.) Set aside.

3 Cut the orange into ¼-inch (6.5mm) slices. Set aside.

4 In a small bowl, whisk together the brown sugar, cornstarch, ginger, and crushed red pepper flakes.

5 Whisk in the orange juice, orange zest, rice vinegar, and soy sauce. Pour the sauce over the chicken and place the orange slices on top.

6 Cover and cook on low for 6 to 8 hours or on high for 4 to 5 hours.

7 When ready to serve, discard the orange slices and serve the chicken hot over rice. Store in the refrigerator for up to 4 days.

VARIATION: Use 2 pounds (1kg) whole chicken thighs, 2 pounds (1kg) drumsticks, or 2 pounds (1kg) wings in place of the chicken breasts. Serve whole with the orange glaze drizzled over the top.

By the Way

Topping the chicken with orange slices not only uses the flesh of the orange after zesting, but also helps keep any exposed chicken moist and infuses the sauce with even more sweet orange flavor.

Moroccan Chicken Thighs

Chicken thighs are cooked between beds of tart and tangy lemon slices, and coated with a bold, Moroccan-style spice blend. The lemon and butter ensure the chicken stays moist and tender.

YIELD	SERVING SIZE	PREP TIME	COOK TIME
6 THIGHS	**1 THIGH**	**5 MINUTES**	**4 TO 8 HOURS**

2 medium lemons, sliced ⅛ inch (3.18mm) thick

6 chicken thighs

1 tsp paprika

½ tsp cumin

¼ tsp turmeric

¼ tsp cayenne

¼ tsp salt

⅛ tsp ground cinnamon

⅛ tsp ground ginger

3 tbsp butter

1 In a 6- to 8-quart (5.5- to 7.5-liter) slow cooker, layer half of the lemon slices and then place the chicken thighs on top.

2 In a small bowl, combine the paprika, cumin, turmeric, cayenne, salt, cinnamon, and ginger. Sprinkle the mixture over the chicken thighs.

3 Cut the butter into 6 pieces and place 1 piece on top of each chicken thigh.

4 Cover and cook on low for 6 to 8 hours or on high for 4 to 5 hours.

5 Serve hot. Store in the refrigerator for up to 4 days.

VARIATION: For **Mexican-Spiced Chicken,** use 4 limes in place of the lemons. Replace the spices listed in step 2 with a blend using 2 teaspoons cumin, 1 teaspoon chili powder, ½ teaspoon cayenne, ½ teaspoon garlic powder, ½ teaspoon salt, and ⅛ teaspoon ground cloves.

TIP: For a crispy skin on the chicken, remove the lemon slices after cooking and place the chicken thighs on a baking sheet. Place under a broiler preheated to high for 2 to 5 minutes or until the skin is crispy. Watch carefully to avoid burning.

Teriyaki Chicken

A sweet, soy-based glaze thickens in the slow cooker and soaks into tender chicken breasts for a succulent and flavorful version of the classic Japanese-inspired dish.

YIELD	SERVING SIZE	PREP TIME	COOK TIME
3 CHICKEN BREASTS	**½ CHICKEN BREAST**	**5 MINUTES**	**4 TO 8 HOURS**

3 (½- to ¾lb [225- to 340g]) boneless, skinless chicken breasts, trimmed

1 tbsp cornstarch

½ cup sugar

½ tsp ground ginger

¼ tsp crushed red pepper flakes

½ cup soy sauce

¼ cup rice vinegar

2 garlic cloves, minced

1 Add the chicken breasts to a 6- to 8-quart (5.5- to 7.5-liter) slow cooker.

2 In a small bowl, combine the cornstarch, sugar, ginger, and crushed red pepper flakes. Whisk in the soy sauce, rice vinegar, and garlic.

3 Pour the glaze over the chicken.

4 Cover and cook on low for 6 to 8 hours or on high for 4 to 5 hours.

5 Slice and serve hot over rice. Store in the refrigerator for up to 4 days.

VARIATION: You can use 2 pounds (1kg) whole thighs, 2 pounds (1kg) drumsticks, or 2 pounds (1kg) wings in place of the chicken breasts. Serve with the glaze drizzled over the top.

By the Way

Cornstarch is used as a thickening agent in this recipe. If mixed with liquid on its own, it can become lumpy, but if you mix the fine-powdered cornstarch with the sugar and spices beforehand, it will easily incorporate into the sauce without clumping.

CHAPTER 8

Pork

Pork soaks up flavors as it cooks, making it a terrific candidate for low and slow cooking. The long cook times of the low and slow method maximizes the amount of flavor the meat can take on. You can cook lean cuts of pork on either high or low heat settings, but tougher cuts work best on low.

Strawberry-Chipotle Barbecue Baby Back Ribs

These tender, fall-off-the-bone ribs are sure to please any meat lover.
The strawberry-chipotle barbecue sauce stews with the ribs for
a succulent, sweet, and spicy bite of delicate, juicy meat.

YIELD	SERVING SIZE	PREP TIME	COOK TIME
2 RACKS	**½ RACK**	**20 MINUTES**	**8 HOURS**

2 tbsp olive oil

1 large sweet onion, diced

2 garlic cloves, minced

2 cups fresh strawberries, hulled

3 chipotle chiles in adobo sauce

1 cup ketchup

⅔ cup brown sugar (light or dark), tightly packed

1 tbsp Worcestershire sauce

2 tsp ground mustard

½ tsp freshly ground black pepper

2 racks pork loin baby back ribs

1 In a large saucepan over medium-high heat, heat the olive oil. Add the onion and sauté, stirring occasionally, for 5 minutes. Add the garlic and sauté for 1 more minute.

2 Stir in the strawberries, chipotle chiles, ketchup, brown sugar, Worcestershire sauce, ground mustard, and black pepper. Increase the heat to high and bring to a boil, then reduce the heat to medium-low and simmer for 10 minutes.

3 Carefully transfer the sauce to a blender, filling the blender pitcher no more than half full. Place the lid securely on the pitcher and loosen the removable fill cap to create a vent for the steam. Purée for 1 to 2 minutes or until smooth. (Note: Pressure buildup can lead to explosions, so always be sure to vent any steam while puréeing.)

4 Add the ribs to a 6- to 8-quart (5.5- to 7.5-liter) slow cooker. (If the racks are too large to fit in your slow cooker, cut them in half.) Pour the sauce over the ribs.

5 Cover and cook on low for 8 hours.

6 Serve hot. Store in the refrigerator for up to 4 days.

TIP: You can give these ribs that extra "grilled" touch by brushing the cooked ribs with additional barbecue sauce and then placing them under a broiler for a few minutes until the sauce caramelizes, bubbles, and darkens. Or you can brush them with the extra sauce, wrap them in aluminum foil, and place them on an outdoor grill for 5 to 7 minutes.

Apple Pork Roast

Sweet apples and onions surround supple pork in this
slow-cooked roast that highlights the flavors of fall.

YIELD	SERVING SIZE	PREP TIME	COOK TIME
3 TO 4 POUNDS	**½ TO ⅓ POUND**	**5 MINUTES**	**6 TO 8 HOURS**
(1.5 TO 2KG)	**(115 TO 150G)**		

3- to 4lb (1.5- to 2kg) pork roast

4 medium apples (any variety), cored, halved, and quartered

½ cup apple juice

2 tbsp brown sugar (light or dark)

1 tsp salt

1 large sweet onion, halved and sliced

1 Add the pork roast to a 6- to 8-quart (5.5- to 7.5-liter) slow cooker.

2 Surround the roast with the apples and then pour the apple juice over the top.

3 Sprinkle the brown sugar and salt over the roast. Top with the onion slices.

4 Cover and cook on low for 6 to 8 hours.

5 Slice and serve hot with the apples and onions. Store in the refrigerator for up to 4 days.

VARIATION: You can use 4 bone-in, thick-cut pork chops in place of the roast in this recipe. The cook time will be the same.

By the Way

You have many choices when it comes to pork roasts. Pork loin and sirloin roasts are leaner cuts that won't shred as easily, allowing you to slice the roast to serve it. Shoulder and butt roasts are more marbled with fat and will shred easily after long, slow cooking.

Dijon-Crusted Pork Tenderloin

The concentrated, tangy flavors of Dijon mustard
form a flavorful crust on this cut of tenderloin.

YIELD	SERVING SIZE	PREP TIME	COOK TIME
8 SLICES	**2 OR 3 SLICES**	**5 MINUTES**	**3 TO 7 HOURS**

1lb (450g) pork tenderloin

½ tsp salt

¼ tsp freshly ground
   black pepper

2 tbsp Dijon mustard

1 Season the tenderloin with the salt and black pepper. Rub the entire surface with the Dijon mustard.

2 Add the tenderloin to a 6- to 8-quart (5.5- to 7.5-liter) slow cooker.

3 Cover and cook on on low for 5 to 7 hours or on high for 3 to 4 hours.

4 Let the tenderloin rest for 10 minutes before cutting into ½-inch (1cm) slices. Serve hot. Store in the refrigerator for up to 4 days.

VARIATION: For **Spicy Crusted Tenderloin,** coat the outside of the meat with 2 tablespoons chipotle chili powder or 3 minced chipotle chiles in adobo sauce, ½ teaspoon garlic powder, ½ teaspoon onion powder, ½ teaspoon salt, and 2 tablespoons brown sugar.

By the Way

Pork tenderloins are quite small, so you can easily double
this recipe. Place the tenderloins in a single layer, side by side
in the slow cooker, and cook as directed.

Hawaiian Kalua Pork

This slow cooker version of the island favorite is tender and moist. The liquid smoke provides the deep pit–smoked flavor, and the salt brings an island taste of the sea.

YIELD	SERVING SIZE	PREP TIME	COOK TIME
3 TO 4 POUNDS **(1.5 TO 2KG)**	**¼ TO ⅓ POUND** **(115 TO 150G)**	**5 MINUTES**	**8 HOURS**

3- to 4lb (1.5- to 2kg) boneless pork butt or shoulder roast

3 tbsp liquid smoke

1 tbsp sea salt

1 Add the pork roast to a 6- to 8-quart (5.5- to 7.5-liter) slow cooker.

2 Pour the liquid smoke over the roast and then season with the sea salt.

3 Cover and cook on low for 8 hours.

4 Use two forks to shred the meat. Serve hot. Store in the refrigerator for up to 4 days.

TIP: For a more authentic flavor, use Hawaiian pink sea salt in place of the sea salt.

By the Way

Kalua refers to a traditional Hawaiian cooking method in which food is cooked in an underground oven. Hot rocks are used as a heat source, and banana leaves provide a lining. The heat is low, the cooking process is long—much like slow cooking—and the food being cooked soaks up a smoky flavor during the cooking process.

Orange-Balsamic Glazed Ham

Making a delicious ham couldn't be any easier than
this vibrant, tangy, and sweet glazed ham.

YIELD	SERVING SIZE	PREP TIME	COOK TIME
1 POUND (450G)	**⅓ TO ½ POUND (150 TO 225G)**	**5 MINUTES**	**5 TO 8 HOURS**

5- to 8lb (2.5- to 4kg) fully cooked, bone-in smoked ham

1 cup orange juice

½ cup balsamic vinegar

½ cup brown sugar (light or dark), tightly packed

1 tsp salt

1 Place the ham, cut side down, in a 6- to 8-quart (5.5- to 7.5-liter) slow cooker.

2 In a medium bowl, whisk together the orange juice, balsamic vinegar, brown sugar, and salt. Pour the glaze over the ham.

3 Cover and cook on low for 5 to 8 hours or approximately 1 hour per pound.

4 Serve hot. Store in the refrigerator for up to 4 days.

TIP: It's important to ensure the ham you buy fits in your slow cooker—the slow cooker lid must rest securely on the rim of the stoneware insert. If in doubt, take a small measuring tape with you to the grocery store and measure the hams to ensure you find one that will fit in your cooker.

Smothered Pork Chops

A flavorful gravy and cooked onions provide the "smothering" gravy for these thick and tender pork chops. Spoon on the gravy for a saucy pork dinner.

YIELD	SERVING SIZE	PREP TIME	COOK TIME
4 CHOPS	**1 CHOP**	**5 MINUTES**	**4 TO 8 HOURS**

4 (½- to 1-inch thick [1- to 2.5cm)] bone-in pork chops

1 tsp salt

½ tsp freshly ground black pepper

1 tbsp cornstarch

1 tbsp water

1 cup chicken broth

2 tsp onion powder

2 tsp garlic powder

2 large sweet onions, halved and sliced

1 Season both sides of the pork chops with the salt and black pepper. Add the chops to a 6- to 8-quart (5.5- to 7.5-liter) slow cooker.

2 In a medium bowl, combine the cornstarch and water. Stir in the chicken broth, onion powder, and garlic powder.

3 Pour the mixture around the pork chops and then top with the onion slices.

4 Cover and cook on low for 6 to 8 hours or on high for 4 to 5 hours.

5 Transfer to a serving dish and top with the gravy and onions. Serve hot. Store in the refrigerator for up to 4 days.

By the Way

Bone-in pork chops are preferable to boneless in this recipe because they're harder to dry out. The bone helps the meat retain moisture and slows the cooking process, resulting in a moist and tender, slow-cooked chop.

Killer Carnitas

This tender, shredded pork packs a bold flavor, thanks to the cumin and chili powder, and the cayenne brings just enough heat to add a little kick. Cooked in a seasoned oil, the meat is super tender and indulgent.

YIELD	SERVING SIZE	PREP TIME	COOK TIME
6 CUPS	**½ CUP**	**10 MINUTES**	**6 TO 8 HOURS**

4lb (2kg) pork butt roast, trimmed and cut into ¼-inch thick (.5cm) slices

2 tbsp ground cumin

1 tbsp chili powder

2 tbsp garlic powder

2 tbsp salt

1½ tbsp cayenne

1 tsp ground cloves

2 cups vegetable oil

2 bay leaves

1 Add the pork slices to a 6- to 8-quart (5.5- to 7.5-liter) slow cooker.

2 In a medium bowl, combine the cumin, chili powder, garlic powder, salt, cayenne, cloves, and vegetable oil.

3 Pour the mixture over the pork pieces and stir to coat. Tuck the bay leaves down into the oil.

4 Cover and cook on low for 6 to 8 hours or until the meat can easily be shredded with a fork.

5 Strain the oil from the meat, remove the bay leaves, and use two forks to shred before serving. Store in the refrigerator for up to 4 days.

VARIATION: Add ½ cup orange juice with the vegetable oil for a regional variation of carnitas.

By the Way

Carnitas, or "little meats," is a popular Mexican braised pork. You can serve the tender, shredded meat as a dish by itself, or use it in tacos, burritos, tamales, or tortas. You don't need much to dress up this flavorful meat—a taco only needs some fresh cilantro, diced onion, and diced tomato on a corn or flour tortilla to bring a big, bold taco bite.

CHAPTER 9

Vegetables

In addition to softening tough cuts of meat, the slow cooker can perfectly cook vegetables, like artichokes and potatoes, that require long cooking times. With a slow cooker and a few hours, you'll get delicious vegetable dishes that even finicky eaters will love.

Stuffed Artichokes

You can get the gourmet taste of stuffed artichokes with the help of the slow cooker. Seasoned breadcrumbs and Parmesan cheese fill the interiors of the artichokes, topping the hearts with buttery goodness.

YIELD	SERVING SIZE	PREP TIME	COOK TIME
4 ARTICHOKES	**1 ARTICHOKE**	**15 MINUTES**	**3 TO 6 HOURS**

4 large whole artichokes

1 cup breadcrumbs

1 cup shredded Parmesan cheese

4 garlic cloves, minced

1 tsp dried basil

¼ tsp salt

½ cup butter, melted

1 Cut off the stems of the artichokes so they can sit upright. Use a pair of kitchen scissors to trim off any sharp leaf tips.

2 Using a large spoon, scoop out and discard the artichoke center chokes or hairs.

3 In a medium bowl, combine the breadcrumbs, Parmesan cheese, garlic, basil, and salt. Stir in the melted butter.

4 Evenly spoon the breadcrumb mixture into the hollowed-out centers of the artichokes.

5 Pour enough water into the bottom of a 6- to 8-quart (5.5- to 7.5-liter) slow cooker to cover the bottom by ½ inch (1 centimeter). Stand the artichokes in the water.

6 Cover and cook on low for 5 to 6 hours or on high for 3 to 4 hours.

7 To eat, use a spoon to scoop down through the breadcrumb mixture and into the heart. As you make your way to the center heart, peel back and eat the flesh from the tips of the leaves by scraping it off with your teeth. Store in the refrigerator for up 4 days.

VARIATION: Add ½ cup chopped sun-dried tomatoes to the breadcrumb mixture.

TIP: The artichokes might start to turn slightly brown after you hollow out the centers. To prevent this, rub the exposed artichoke hearts with a little lemon juice immediately after cutting.

Country-Style Green Beans

The low-and-slow method a slow cooker offers produces soft and tender green beans that are smothered in onion, with just a hint of smoky ham.

YIELD	SERVING SIZE	PREP TIME	COOK TIME
6 CUPS	**1 CUP**	**10 MINUTES**	**6 TO 8 HOURS**

1½lb (680g) fresh green beans, ends trimmed

1 medium yellow onion, diced

½ tsp salt

6 garlic cloves, minced

¼ tsp crushed red pepper flakes

¼ tsp freshly ground black pepper

8oz (225g) ham hock

1 Add the green beans, onion, salt, garlic, crushed red pepper flakes, and black pepper to a 4- to 6-quart (4- to 5.5-liter) slow cooker. Toss to combine.

2 Using a knife, make several slashes across the surface of the ham hock. Add the hock to the slow cooker, burrowing it down into the green beans.

3 Cover and cook on low for 6 to 8 hours.

4 Remove and discard the ham hock before serving. Store in the refrigerator for up to 4 days.

VARIATION: For a vegetarian version, omit the ham hock.

TIP: When purchasing fresh green beans, avoid beans that are shriveled or limp. To prepare them for cooking, either snap or trim off the ends. You can then either snap the beans in half or leave them long.

Creamed Corn

In this easy, slow-cooked dish, simple corn becomes a
decadent treat with a creamy texture and a sweet taste.

YIELD	SERVING SIZE	PREP TIME	COOK TIME
6 CUPS	**½ CUP**	**5 MINUTES**	**2 TO 3 HOURS**

6 cups frozen corn kernels,
  thawed

1 cup reduced fat (2%) milk

1 tbsp sugar

½ tsp salt

8oz (225g) cream cheese,
  cut into ½-inch (1.25cm)
  cubes

½ cup butter, cut into
  ½-inch (1.25cm) cubes

1 Combine the corn, milk, sugar, and salt in a 4- to 6-quart
(4- to 5.5-liter) slow cooker.

2 Place the cream cheese and butter cubes on top of the corn.

3 Cover and cook on high for 2 to 3 hours.

4 Stir before serving hot. Store in the refrigerator for up
to 4 days.

By the Way

Wondering why you should wait 2 or 3 hours for this recipe to
cook when you could just open a can of creamed corn? Canned
cream-style corn is partially puréed to create a soupy sweet corn
mixture with the "milk," or juice from the corn. With this recipe,
the butter and cream cheese combine to create a truly decadent
cream base for the sweet corn. The result is much more
delicious than anything that comes from a can.

Roasted Summer Vegetable Medley

These summer vegetables have a smoky, straight-off-the-grill flavor, thanks to liquid smoke. This super easy side is perfect for a summer barbecue or picnic.

YIELD	SERVING SIZE	PREP TIME	COOK TIME
4 CUPS	**¾ CUP**	**5 MINUTES**	**2 TO 4 HOURS**

1 pint (550g) cherry tomatoes

1 medium zucchini, ends removed, halved, and sliced

1 medium yellow onion, cut into 1-inch (2.5cm) chunks

2 large red bell peppers, ribs and seeds removed, and cut into 1-inch (2.5cm) chunks

½ tsp salt

¼ tsp freshly ground black pepper

2 tbsp olive oil

1 tsp liquid smoke

1 Add the cherry tomatoes, zucchini, yellow onion, and bell peppers to a 3- to 6-quart (3- to 5.5-liter) slow cooker.

2 Season with the salt and black pepper, pour in the olive oil and liquid smoke, and toss to coat.

3 Cover and cook on high for 2 hours or on low for 3 to 4 hours, or just until the vegetables are tender.

4 Serve hot. Store in the refrigerator for up to 4 days.

By the Way

Zucchini is abundant during the summer months, and home gardeners often give it away to friends and neighbors by the bushel. The thick stem on the top end of the zucchini is inedible and should be cut off, but it's better that the skins be left on for slow cooking because the thick skin holds the soft flesh together.

Creamy Whipped Potatoes

Butter, buttermilk, and cream cheese add to the flavor and creaminess of these slow cooker mashed potatoes that are whipped to a deliciously smooth texture.

YIELD	SERVING SIZE	PREP TIME	COOK TIME
2 CUPS	**1 CUP**	**10 MINUTES**	**4 TO 7 HOURS**

5 large russet potatoes, peeled and cubed

6 cups chicken broth

½ cup butter

8oz (225g) cream cheese

1 cup buttermilk

1½ tsp salt

¼ cup sliced green onions, green parts only (optional)

1 Place the potatoes in a 6- to 8-quart (5.5- to 7.5-liter) slow cooker. Pour in the chicken broth.

2 Cover and cook on low for 5 to 6 hours or on high 3 to 4 hours, or until the potatoes are tender.

3 Drain any excess liquid from the potatoes. Using an electric mixer on high speed, whip the potatoes for about 2 minutes in the slow cooker.

4 Add the butter, cream cheese, buttermilk, and salt on top of potatoes.

5 Cover and cook on high for 1 more hour to allow the butter and cream cheese to melt.

6 Whip the potatoes for 30 seconds and then garnish with green onions (if using) to serve. Stir and serve hot. Store in the refrigerator for up to 4 days

VARIATION: For **Garlic Whipped Potatoes,** add 4 cloves minced garlic with the butter.

By the Way

Whipping the potatoes instead of mashing them produces a much smoother texture with little to no chunks. The cream cheese and butter in this recipe help create a smooth and creamy texture.

Honey Mustard–Roasted Potatoes

In this buttery honey mustard potato dish, red potatoes are coated in the acidic and slightly spicy flavors of Dijon mustard, while honey adds a nice, sweet note.

YIELD	SERVING SIZE	PREP TIME	COOK TIME
6 CUPS	**1 CUP**	**10 MINUTES**	**3 TO 7 HOURS**

8 medium red potatoes, cut into 1-inch (2.5cm) pieces

1 medium yellow onion, diced

¼ cup butter

¼ cup honey

1 tbsp Dijon mustard

1 tsp dried oregano

1 tsp salt

½ tsp freshly ground black pepper

1 Add the red potatoes, onion, butter, honey, Dijon mustard, oregano, salt, and black pepper to a 6- to 8-quart (5.5- to 7.5-liter) slow cooker. Toss to combine.

2 Cover and cook on low for 6 to 7 hours or on high for 3 to 4 hours, or until the potatoes are tender.

3 Stir and serve hot. Store in the refrigerator for up to 4 days.

By the Way

Yellow onions and sweet onions are the most versatile varieties, and both work really well in the slow cooker. Yellow onions produce a mild onion flavor after the slow cooking process, sweet onions produce a mild onion flavor plus a slightly sweet note, and white onions produce a sharper onion flavor and don't soften as much. Red onions are best eaten raw.

Ratatouille

This version of the traditional French dish slow cooks fresh and flavorful veggies to delicious goodness, with very little additional flavoring. Garlic, salt, and black pepper are enough to showcase the natural flavors of the vegetables.

YIELD	SERVING SIZE	PREP TIME	COOK TIME
6 CUPS	**1 CUP**	**15 MINUTES**	**2 TO 5 HOURS**

1 medium eggplant, peeled and diced

1 medium zucchini, diced

1 large green bell pepper, ribs and seeds removed, and diced

2 medium tomatoes, hulled and diced

1 medium yellow onion, diced

8oz (225g) can tomato sauce

4 garlic cloves, minced

1 tsp salt

½ tsp freshly ground black pepper

1 Add the eggplant, zucchini, bell pepper, tomatoes, onion, tomato sauce, garlic, salt, and black pepper to a 4- to 6-quart (4- to 5.5-liter) slow cooker.

2 Cover and cook on high for 2 to 3 hours or on low for 4 to 5 hours. Store in the refrigerator for up to 4 days.

VARIATION: Instead of dicing the ingredients, you can slice them thinly and alternate slices of the various vegetables to create a layered version of the dish.

TIP: To create a crostini, simply top a slice of a crusty French loaf bread with a spoonful of the ratatouille. You can even add a bit of shredded Parmesan on top and toast it under a broiler for a few minutes or until just browned.

By the Way

Ratatouille is usually served as a side dish, but it also can be a main dish, especially when accompanied by bread or pasta.

Corn on the Cob

Summertime corn on the cob has never been easier! Simply season, wrap, and cook, and you'll get sweet, butter-soaked corn that's ready to eat right out of the slow cooker.

YIELD	SERVING SIZE	PREP TIME	COOK TIME
6 EARS	**1 EAR**	**10 MINUTES**	**2 TO 5 HOURS**

6 medium ears of corn, shucked

6 tbsp butter, softened

½ tsp salt

½ tsp freshly ground black pepper

1 Tear off 6 (12-inch [15cm]) sheets of aluminum foil. Place 1 ear of corn on each sheet.

2 Smear 1 tablespoon of the softened butter over each ear and season with salt and black pepper.

3 Tightly wrap each ear in the foil. Place the wrapped ears in a 6- to 8-quart (5.5- to 7.5-liter) slow cooker.

4 Cover and cook on low for 4 to 5 hours or on high for 2 to 3 hours.

5 Serve hot. Store in the refrigerator for up to 4 days.

VARIATIONS: For **Chili and Lime Corn on the Cob,** season each buttered cob with ½ teaspoon chili powder and then squeeze lime juice over top before wrapping. For **Curry Corn on the Cob,** season each buttered cob with ½ teaspoon curry powder and ⅛ teaspoon salt before wrapping.

TIP: When choosing ears of corn, look for ears with bright green husks. Peel back a little of the husk, exposing just the tip of the cob, to check the corn kernels. The kernels should have a fresh yellow or white color and be nice and plump. Avoid ears with dry or discolored kernels.

Scalloped Potatoes

Thin-sliced potatoes bask in a creamy sauce enhanced
by the earthy flavor of nutmeg. The slow cooker is the perfect
cooking tool for this tender and creamy potato classic.

YIELD	SERVING SIZE	PREP TIME	COOK TIME
6 CUPS	**1 CUP**	**10 MINUTES**	**3 TO 8 HOURS**

2 large russet potatoes, peeled and cut into thin slices approximately ⅛ inch (3mm) thick

1 cup heavy cream

2 garlic cloves, minced

½ cup freshly grated Parmesan cheese

½ tsp ground nutmeg

½ tsp salt

¼ tsp freshly ground black pepper

1 Place the potato slices in a large bowl. Pour the heavy cream over the potatoes.

2 Gently stir in the garlic, Parmesan cheese, nutmeg, salt, and black pepper to coat the potatoes. Pour the potatoes into a 6- to 8-quart (5.5- to 7.5-liter) slow cooker.

3 Cover and cook on low for 6 to 8 hours or on high for 3 to 4 hours.

4 Serve hot. Store in the refrigerator for up to 4 days.

VARIATION: For extra cheesiness, add 1 cup grated cheddar cheese on top during the last hour of cooking.

TIP: The easiest way to slice or scallop potatoes is using a food processor. A mandoline slicer is also handy and easily creates thin, even slices. If you don't have either of these tools, try using the slicing side of a cheese grater, rubbing the potatoes against the slicer for thin slices. A knife is the most difficult tool to use because slicing potatoes thin enough to be scalloped requires a very sharp knife and precise cutting.

Cheesy Bacon and Ranch Potatoes

Potatoes are coated with traditional ranch dressing spices, topped with bacon, and finished with cheese and buttermilk for a creamy and flavorful potato side.

YIELD	SERVING SIZE	PREP TIME	COOK TIME
6 CUPS	**1 CUP**	**15 MINUTES**	**3 TO 7 HOURS**

1lb (450g) bacon

8 medium red potatoes, cut into 1-inch (2.5cm) cubes

1 medium yellow onion, diced

1 tbsp dried parsley

1 tsp dried dill

1 tsp salt

½ tsp garlic powder

½ tsp onion powder

½ tsp dried chives

¼ tsp freshly ground black pepper

2 tbsp olive oil

2 cups shredded cheddar cheese

½ cup buttermilk

½ cup sliced green onions, green parts only

1 Place the bacon in a room-temperature skillet over medium heat. Cook for 10 minutes and then flip the bacon and cook for 7 to 10 minutes more or until crispy. Transfer to a paper towel–covered plate to drain.

2 Add the red potatoes, onion, parsley, dill, salt, garlic powder, onion powder, chives, black pepper, and olive oil to a 6- to 8-quart (5.5- to 7.5-liter) slow cooker. Toss to combine.

3 Crumble the cooked bacon over the top of the potato mixture.

4 Cover and cook on low for 6 to 7 hours or on high for 3 to 4 hours, or until the potatoes are tender.

5 Stir the cheddar cheese and buttermilk into the hot potatoes, top with the green onions, and serve hot. Store in the refrigerator for up to 4 days.

VARIATION: Omit the bacon for a vegetarian-friendly version.

By the Way

Adding bacon to a hot pan can result in scorching. Starting the bacon in a cold pan lets the fat loosen up and ensures the bacon cooks more evenly. Cooking the bacon until crisp before adding it to the slow cooker keeps the bacon from getting too soggy during the slow cooking process. In this dish, the cooked bacon is crumbled over the top to help it remain crisp.

Southern Collard Greens

Collard greens are cooked low and slow in this spicy southern dish. The leafy greens are slowly simmered in a flavorful broth until the leaves are tasty and tender.

YIELD	SERVING SIZE	PREP TIME	COOK TIME
3 CUPS	**½ CUP**	**5 MINUTES**	**2 TO 6 HOURS**

1 lb (450g) collard greens, rinsed and drained, stems removed, and roughly chopped

1 medium yellow onion, diced

2 garlic cloves, minced

1 tsp salt

½ tsp freshly ground black pepper

½ tsp crushed red pepper flakes

3 cups chicken broth

1 In a 4- to 6-quart (4- to 5.5-liter) slow cooker, combine the collard greens, onion, garlic, salt, black pepper, and crushed red pepper flakes. Toss to coat and then pour in the chicken broth.

2 Cover and cook on low for 4 to 6 hours or on high for 2 to 3 hours.

3 Serve hot. Store in the refrigerator for up to 4 days.

VARIATION: For a smoky ham flavor, add a ham hock. Remove and discard the hock before serving.

By the Way

Collard greens are in the same family as cabbage and broccoli. The leaves are quite thick, which means they need a long cook time to become tender. The stems, although edible, are particularly tough and can end up chewy, so they're best removed with a sharp knife.

Sweet Potato Casserole

Buttery sweet potatoes are seasoned with sugar and vanilla, and topped with a pecan streusel. The combination of crunchy crust and creamy whipped sweet potatoes almost makes this favorite side dish a dessert.

YIELD	SERVING SIZE	PREP TIME	COOK TIME
6 CUPS	**1 CUP**	**15 MINUTES**	**5 TO 8 HOURS**

6 medium sweet potatoes, peeled and cubed

6 cups water

½ cup sugar

½ tsp salt

4 tbsp butter

½ cup reduced fat (2%) milk

½ tsp pure vanilla extract

½ cup brown sugar (light or dark), firmly packed

⅛ cup all-purpose flour

3 tbsp butter, softened

½ cup chopped pecans

1 Place the sweet potatoes in a 6- to 8-quart (5.5- to 7.5-liter) slow cooker. Pour in the water.

2 Cover and cook on low for 5 to 6 hours or on high for 3 to 4 hours.

3 Drain any excess liquid from the sweet potatoes. Using an electric mixer on high speed, whip the potatoes for about 2 minutes or until smooth. Whip in the sugar, salt, butter, milk, and vanilla extract. Use a wooden spoon to smooth the whipped potatoes into the bottom of the slow cooker.

4 In a small bowl, use a pastry cutter to cut together the brown sugar, flour, and butter until the mixture resembles cornmeal. Stir in the chopped pecans and then sprinkle the mixture over the sweet potatoes.

5 Cover and cook on high for 2 more hours.

6 Serve hot. Store in the refrigerator for up to 4 days.

By the Way

A pastry cutter is a handheld kitchen tool consisting of several strips of parallel blades attached to a handle. It's most often used to cut fat into flour. If you don't have a pastry cutter, you can use two butter knives instead. Hold one butter knife in each hand with the tips in the dough, crossed near the handles. Quickly cut the knives parallel to each other, moving them in opposite directions. Repeat quickly, moving throughout the dough, cutting the butter into the flour and brown sugar.

Roasted Beets 'n' Sweets

The sweet flavors of fresh beets, sweet potatoes, and sweet onions are combined in this savory side. Garlic and black pepper counteract the sweetness, making this a balanced and flavorful dish.

YIELD	SERVING SIZE	PREP TIME	COOK TIME
6 CUPS	**1 CUP**	**15 MINUTES**	**3 TO 7 HOURS**

3 medium fresh beets, tops removed, peeled, and cubed

3 medium sweet potatoes, peeled and cubed

1 large sweet onion, diced

2 tbsp olive oil

1 tbsp brown sugar (light or dark)

1 tsp garlic powder

1 tsp salt

½ tsp freshly ground black pepper

1 Add the beets, sweet potatoes, and onion to a 6- to 8-quart (5.5- to 7.5-liter) slow cooker.

2 Pour in the olive oil and then stir in the brown sugar, garlic powder, salt, and black pepper.

3 Cover and cook on low for 6 to 7 hours or on high for 3 to 4 hours, or until the potatoes and beets are tender.

4 Serve hot. Store in the refrigerator for up to 4 days.

By the Way

Fresh beets will stain everything they touch. Pink hands and cutting boards are common after cooking beets, as are stained shirts. Most stains can be rinsed away easily, but if this is a concern, wear gloves to protect your hands and an apron to protect your clothes.

CHAPTER 10

Pastas, Rice, and Beans

Whether it's a main dish or a side dish, the slow cooker makes cooking pastas, rice, and beans so incredibly simple. Note that in some of the pasta recipes in this chapter, the noodles are cooked directly in the slow cooker, while others call for cooking the pasta on the stovetop. For pastas that are traditionally baked—like lasagna or macaroni & cheese—the noodles can simply be cooked in the slow cooker. However, sauce-based dishes are best served over freshly cooked pasta to avoid mushy noodles.

Classic Italian Lasagna

Layers of savory sausage and ground beef, a melty combination of four different cheeses, lasagna noodles, and Italian spices make this classic dish simple with the ease of the slow cooker.

YIELD	SERVING SIZE	PREP TIME	COOK TIME
8 SLICES	**1 SLICE**	**20 MINUTES**	**4 TO 6 HOURS**

1lb (450g) ground beef

1lb (450g) ground pork sausage

1 medium yellow onion, diced

4 garlic cloves, minced

1 tsp salt

1 tsp dried basil

1 tsp dried oregano

4 cups marinara sauce

16oz (450g) ricotta cheese

1 large egg

1 tbsp dried parsley

10 oven-ready lasagna pasta sheets

3 cups shredded mozzarella cheese, divided

6 slices provolone cheese

½ cup shredded Parmesan cheese

1 Add the ground beef, ground sausage, and onion to a large skillet over medium-high heat. Cook, stirring occasionally, for 7 to 10 minutes or until the meat is browned. Drain any excess fat from the pan. Stir in the garlic, salt, basil, oregano, and marinara sauce.

2 Scoop a spoonful of the sauce mixture into the bottom of a 6- to 8-quart (5.5- to 7.5-liter) oval slow cooker. Use the back of the spoon to spread the mixture across the bottom of the slow cooker.

3 In a small bowl, whisk together the ricotta cheese, egg, and parsley.

4 Place 2 lasagna pasta sheets parallel in the bottom of the slow cooker. Break a third pasta sheet in half and place the pieces at the ends of the oval. (The pasta sheets will expand as they cook.) Top with a third of the ricotta mixture, followed by a quarter of the sauce mixture, and 1 cup mozzarella.

5 Next, layer 3 pasta sheets as before, followed by a third of the ricotta mixture, a quarter of the sauce mixture, and the provolone cheese slices. Layer 3 more pasta sheets as before and top with the remaining ricotta cheese, a quarter of the sauce mixture, and 1 cup mozzarella.

6 Top with the remaining 3 pasta sheets and remaining sauce mixture. Sprinkle with the remaining 1 cup mozzarella and Parmesan cheese.

7 Cover and cook on low for 4 to 6 hours.

8 Cut into 8 slices and serve hot. Store in the refrigerator for up to 4 days.

VARIATION: For **Spinach Lasagna**, evenly divide 10 ounces (285g) frozen spinach that has been thawed and drained over the top of each ricotta layer.

Cheesy Ravioli Casserole

In this versatile comfort food recipe, tender ravioli are smothered between gooey layers of cheese and finished off with tangy marinara sauce.

YIELD	SERVING SIZE	PREP TIME	COOK TIME
2 CUPS	**1 CUP**	**5 MINUTES**	**5 TO 6 HOURS**

50oz (1.5kg) frozen ravioli, divided

3 cups shredded mozzarella cheese, divided

1 cup shredded Parmesan cheese, divided

3 cups marinara sauce

1 Place one third of the ravioli in a 6- to 8-quart (5.5- to 7.5-liter) slow cooker. Top with 1 cup mozzarella cheese and ⅓ cup Parmesan cheese.

2 Create two more layers in the same fashion, each with a third of the ravioli topped with 1 cup mozzarella and ⅓ cup Parmesan.

3 Pour the marinara sauce over the pasta.

4 Cover and cook on low for 5 to 6 hours or until the cheeses are melted and the ravioli are heated through.

5 Serve hot. Store in the refrigerator for up to 4 days.

VARIATION: In a large skillet over medium-high heat, heat 1 tablespoon olive oil. Add 1 medium yellow onion, diced, and 4 cloves minced garlic, and sauté for 5 to 7 minutes. Layer the sautéed onion and garlic on top of the pasta in step 2.

By the Way

Simple meat and cheese-filled ravioli are the most common varieties, but you also can find more gourmet flavors like mushroom, spinach, butternut squash, or even lobster. Any of these can be used in this recipe. If you're using fresh (not frozen) ravioli in this recipe, reduce the cook time by 1 to 2 hours.

Creamy Mushroom Risotto

This traditionally time-intensive creamy rice dish is simple in the slow cooker.
Arborio rice soaks in the chicken broth to create a creamy starch sauce,
and the dish is served topped with freshly sautéed mushrooms.

YIELD	SERVING SIZE	PREP TIME	COOK TIME
6 CUPS	**1 CUP**	**10 MINUTES**	**2 TO 3 HOURS**

6 cups chicken broth

1½ cups Arborio rice

½ medium yellow onion, diced

1 tsp salt

½ tsp freshly ground black pepper

4 tbsp butter

⅛ cup grated Parmesan cheese

2 tbsp olive oil

16oz (450g) mushrooms, sliced

1 Combine the chicken broth, Arborio rice, onion, salt, and black pepper in a 4- to 6-quart (4- to 5.5-liter) slow cooker.

2 Cover and cook on high for 2 to 3 hours or until the rice has absorbed the broth.

3 Transfer the rice to a large bowl and stir in the butter and Parmesan cheese. Stir until the Parmesan is melted.

4 In a large skillet over high heat, heat the olive oil. Add the mushrooms and sauté, stirring occasionally, for 3 to 5 minutes.

5 Top the rice with the cooked mushrooms and serve hot. Store in the refrigerator for up to 4 days.

By the Way

The mushrooms are added at the end of this recipe to keep them from becoming soggy. Until they're added, this recipe is a nice, easily adaptable base recipe for other risottos. You can also add vegetables like asparagus, broccoli, or fennel, and then steam them on top of the rice.

Spaghetti and Meatballs

Large and flavorful meatballs are slowly cooked in a homemade spaghetti sauce. Making this classic dish from scratch is simplified using the low-and-slow method a slow cooker offers.

YIELD	SERVING SIZE	PREP TIME	COOK TIME
12 CUPS	**2 CUPS**	**15 MINUTES**	**3 TO 4 HOURS**

2 (15oz [420g]) cans diced tomatoes, drained

2 tbsp tomato paste

½ medium yellow onion, diced

4 garlic cloves, minced and divided

1½ tsp salt, divided

1 tsp sugar

2 tsp dried basil, divided

½ tsp freshly ground black pepper

1lb (450g) lean ground beef

⅓ cup dried breadcrumbs

¼ cup grated Parmesan cheese

½ tsp crushed red pepper flakes

3 tbsp reduced fat (2%) milk

2 tbsp Worcestershire sauce

1lb (450g) uncooked spaghetti

1 In a blender or food processor fitted with an S blade, purée the tomatoes, tomato paste, onion, 2 cloves garlic, 1 teaspoon salt, sugar, 1 teaspoon basil, and black pepper until smooth. Pour the tomato sauce into a 6- to 8-quart (5.5- to 7.5-liter) slow cooker.

2 In a medium bowl, combine the ground beef, breadcrumbs, Parmesan cheese, remaining garlic, remaining 1 teaspoon basil, remaining ½ teaspoon salt, crushed red pepper flakes, milk, and Worcestershire sauce. Using your hands, knead the mixture until well combined and then form into 12 meatballs. Place the meatballs into the sauce in the slow cooker.

3 Cover and cook on high for 3 to 4 hours.

4 Cook the spaghetti according to the package directions.

5 Serve the spaghetti hot, topped with sauce and meatballs. Store in the refrigerator for up to 4 days.

TIP: Making a large batch of **Homemade Spaghetti Sauce** is simple in the slow cooker. In a 6- to 8-quart (5.5- to 7.5-liter) slow cooker, combine 10 (14oz [400g]) cans diced tomatoes or 10 pounds (4.5kg) fresh Roma tomatoes, peeled and cored; ¼ cup olive oil; 3 medium yellow onions, diced; 10 cloves garlic, minced; 1 tablespoon salt; 1 tablespoon sugar; 3 tablespoons dried basil; and 1 teaspoon black pepper. Cover and cook on low for 4 to 6 hours. Transfer in small batches to a blender or food processor fitted with an S blade. Purée until smooth or blend in the slow cooker using an immersion blender. Divide the sauce and freeze in resealable plastic freezer bags.

Mexican Refried Beans

Refried beans are a staple side in Mexican cuisine. Seasoned with onion, garlic, and jalapeño, and given a richness from butter, these beans are a tasty, flavorful dish.

YIELD	SERVING SIZE	PREP TIME	COOK TIME
6 CUPS	**½ CUP**	**10 MINUTES**	**8 TO 10 HOURS**

3 cups dry pinto beans, sorted to remove any debris or damaged beans

1 tsp salt

1 medium yellow onion, diced

4 garlic cloves, minced

1 jalapeño, stemmed and minced

9 cups water

½ cup butter

1 Add the beans to a 6- to 8-quart (5.5- to 7.5-liter) slow cooker.

2 Stir in the salt, onion, garlic, and jalapeño, and then pour in the water.

3 Cover and cook on low for 8 to 10 hours.

4 Transfer the cooked beans to a colander to drain.

5 In a food processor fitted with an S blade, purée the beans, or mash by hand with a potato masher.

6 Stir in the butter until completely melted.

7 Serve hot. Store in the refrigerator for up to 4 days.

VARIATION: For a fat-free version, omit the butter.

TIP: Traditionally, refried beans are made by cooking the beans and then frying them in lard with spices. If desired, you can use an equal amount of lard in place of the butter to add a more authentic flavor.

Secret Ingredient Macaroni and Cheese

A creamy cheddar cheese sauce envelops elbow macaroni pasta in this slow cooked home-style favorite. The not-so-secret ingredient, cayenne hot sauce, enhances the flavor of the cheddar without adding much heat.

YIELD	SERVING SIZE	PREP TIME	COOK TIME
8 CUPS	**1 CUP**	**5 MINUTES**	**2 TO 3 HOURS**

½ cup butter, melted

½ cup all-purpose flour

1 tsp salt

1½ tsp ground mustard

1½ tsp onion powder

½ tsp white pepper

5 cups reduced fat (2%) milk

2 tbsp cayenne hot sauce

1lb (450g) dry elbow macaroni pasta

2½ cups shredded sharp cheddar cheese

1 In a large bowl, whisk together the butter, flour, salt, ground mustard, onion powder, and white pepper to form paste. Slowly whisk in the milk and cayenne hot sauce.

2 Add the elbow macaroni and cheddar cheese to a 6- to 8-quart (5.5- to 7.5-liter) slow cooker. Pour in the milk mixture and stir to combine, using the spoon to pat down the macaroni so it's covered in the sauce.

3 Cover and cook on low for 2 to 3 hours or until the milk is absorbed and the pasta is cooked.

4 Serve hot. Store in the refrigerator for up to 4 days.

VARIATION: For **Bacon Mac and Cheese,** add 1 pound (450g) cooked and crumbled bacon just before serving.

TIP: It's all too easy to overcook pasta in the slow cooker, so be sure to check the macaroni at the lowest end of the cook time range to see if it's done.

By the Way

Cayenne hot sauce (also called cayenne pepper hot sauce) is most often used for buffalo wings. You can find it in grocery stores in the condiment section.

Brown Rice and Black Bean Casserole

Hearty brown rice is mixed with black beans, zucchini, carrots, and mushrooms in this healthy dish. Serve as a main course or a side.

YIELD	SERVING SIZE	PREP TIME	COOK TIME
6 CUPS	**1 CUP**	**10 MINUTES**	**3 TO 4 HOURS**

1½ cups long-grain brown rice

3 cups vegetable broth

1 tbsp olive oil

1 tsp ground cumin

3 garlic cloves, minced

1 medium yellow onion, diced

15oz (420g) can black beans, drained and rinsed

4oz (110g) can diced green chiles, with liquid

1 medium zucchini, ends trimmed and diced

3 large carrots, peeled and shredded

8oz (225g) button mushrooms, sliced

2 cups shredded mozzarella cheese

1 Add the brown rice to a 6- to 8-quart (5.5- to 7.5-liter) slow cooker. Pour in the vegetable broth and olive oil, and season with the cumin and garlic.

2 Top the rice mixture with the onion, black beans, green chiles, zucchini, and carrots. Layer the button mushrooms on top.

3 Cover and cook on high for 3 to 4 hours or until the rice is cooked and the liquids are absorbed.

4 Top the hot rice with the mozzarella cheese and let it melt.

5 Serve hot. Store in the refrigerator for up to 4 days.

VARIATION: Cut 2 pounds (1kg) boneless, skinless chicken breasts into bite-sized pieces and then layer the pieces on top of the rice. (Be sure to check the chicken for doneness before serving.)

By the Way

The hearty texture of brown rice makes it stand up really well in slow cooking. Some varieties of white rice can break down and become mushy during slow cooking.

Spanish Rice

Tomatoes and chili powder give this rice dish its bright red color.
Onions, bell peppers, green chiles, and garlic give it a flavor reminiscent
of salsa, making it a perfect partner with other Mexican dishes.

YIELD	SERVING SIZE	PREP TIME	COOK TIME
6 CUPS	**1 CUP**	**5 MINUTES**	**2 TO 3 HOURS**

1 cup long-grain white rice

2 cups chicken broth

1 tsp salt

1 tsp chili powder

1 medium yellow onion, diced

1 large green bell pepper, ribs and seeds removed, and diced

4oz (110g) can diced green chiles, with liquid

15oz (420g) can diced tomatoes, with liquid

3 garlic cloves, minced

1 Add the rice to a 4- to 6-quart (4- to 5.5-liter) slow cooker.

2 Pour in the chicken broth, season with the salt and chili powder, and stir to combine.

3 Layer in the onion, bell pepper, and green chiles (with liquid), and then top with the tomatoes (with liquid) and garlic.

4 Cover and cook on high for 2 to 3 hours or until the rice is cooked through.

5 Stir to combine and serve hot. Store in the refrigerator for up to 4 days.

By the Way

This dish doesn't come from Spain—it's actually native to the southwestern United States, where it's usually served as an accompaniment to Mexican cuisine. The name references the language spoken in Mexico rather than the country of origin. Similar dishes are served in Mexico under various names, but most commonly it's just referred to as rice.

Tri-Tip Beef Stroganoff

A creamy, dark mushroom sauce coats tender beef tri-tip in this
classic pasta recipe served over egg noodles. The meat is the highlight
of the dish, practically falling apart with slow-cooked tenderness.

YIELD	SERVING SIZE	PREP TIME	COOK TIME
12 CUPS	**2 CUPS**	**5 MINUTES**	**8 HOURS**

2lb (1kg) tri-tip beef roast

1 tsp salt

½ tsp freshly ground
   black pepper

1 tbsp cornstarch

2 cups beef broth, divided

1 medium yellow onion,
   diced

8oz (225g) mushrooms,
   sliced

¾ cup sour cream

¼ cup sliced green onions
   (green parts only)

1lb (450g) egg noodles

1 Place the roast in the bottom of a 6- to 8-quart (5.5- to 7.5-liter)
slow cooker. Season with the salt and black pepper.

2 In a small bowl, combine the cornstarch with 1 tablespoon of
beef broth, then stir the cornstarch mixture into the remaining
beef broth and pour around the roast.

3 Top the roast with the onion and mushrooms.

4 Cover and cook on low for 8 hours.

5 Remove the roast from the slow cooker and cut into bite-size
chunks. Return the meat to the slow cooker, stir in the sour cream,
and top with the green onions.

6 Cook the egg noodles according to the package directions.

7 Serve the meat and sauce hot over the top of the cooked egg
noodles. Store in the refrigerator for up to 4 days.

By the Way

Keeping the mushrooms on top of the meat and
out of the liquid prevents them from getting
soggy during the slow cooking process.

Un-Fried Rice

In this easy, slow-cooked dish, you get all the sesame and soy flavors of restaurant-style fried rice without the frying. Carrots and peas add color and flavor to this tasty side.

YIELD	SERVING SIZE	PREP TIME	COOK TIME
6 CUPS	**1 CUP**	**10 MINUTES**	**2 TO 3 HOURS**

2 cups long-grain white rice

4 cups water

2 tbsp olive oil

2 tbsp soy sauce

1 tbsp toasted sesame oil

1 medium yellow onion, diced

4 medium carrots, peeled and diced

½ cup frozen peas, thawed

1 Add the rice, water, olive oil, soy sauce, and sesame oil to a 6- to 8-quart (5.5- to 7.5-liter) slow cooker.

2 Sprinkle the onion, carrots, and peas on top of the rice mixture.

3 Cover and cook on high for 2 to 3 hours or until the rice is cooked through and the liquids have been absorbed.

4 Serve hot. Store in the refrigerator for up to 4 days.

VARIATION: If desired, crack 1 or 2 eggs on top of the cooked rice and cook on high for 1 more hour or until the egg is cooked through. Stir and serve.

By the Way

Sesame oil is derived from sesame seeds. Toasted sesame oil comes from toasted sesame seeds and has a strong, nutty flavor. You can find both regular and toasted versions in the international sections of most well-stocked grocery stores, near items like soy sauce.

White Beans and Pancetta

White beans and salty pancetta are cooked together in this subtle yet flavorful bean dish. This side pairs nicely with Italian meals.

YIELD	SERVING SIZE	PREP TIME	COOK TIME
6 CUPS	**1 CUP**	**10 MINUTES**	**8 TO 10 HOURS**

2 cups dry Great Northern beans, sorted to remove any debris or damaged beans

8 cups chicken broth

½ tsp salt

4oz (110g) diced pancetta

1 medium yellow onion, diced

4 garlic cloves, minced

1 Add the beans to a 6- to 8-quart (5.5- to 7.5-liter) slow cooker. Pour in the chicken broth and stir in the salt.

2 In a large skillet over medium-high heat, cook the pancetta and onion, stirring occasionally, for 5 to 7 minutes. Add the garlic during the last minute of cooking.

3 Transfer the pancetta and onion to the slow cooker. Stir to combine.

4 Cover and cook on low for 8 to 10 hours.

5 Serve hot. Store in the refrigerator for up to 4 days.

VARIATION: For an earthy flavor, stir in 2 tablespoons dried rosemary with the garlic.

By the Way

Pancetta is an Italian bacon. Although it's cut from the same part of the pig as regular bacon, the difference comes in the curing: bacon is smoked, whereas pancetta is not. The two can be used interchangeably in recipes; using bacon will add a smoky element to a dish.

White Vegetable Lasagna

A homemade cheese-filled white sauce is the foundation for this layered vegetable lasagna that features the flavors of artichoke, spinach, and sun-dried tomatoes.

YIELD	SERVING SIZE	PREP TIME	COOK TIME
8 SLICES	**1 SLICE**	**20 MINUTES**	**4 TO 6 HOURS**

½ cup butter

1 medium yellow onion, diced

2 garlic cloves, minced

½ cup all-purpose flour

1 tsp salt

2 cups vegetable broth

1½ cups reduced fat (2%) milk

3 cups shredded mozzarella cheese, divided

1 tsp dried basil

1 tsp dried oregano

½ tsp freshly ground black pepper

10oz (285g) frozen spinach, thawed and thoroughly drained

2 cups chopped artichoke hearts

½ cup sun-dried tomatoes, roughly chopped

10 oven-ready lasagna pasta sheets

16oz (450g) ricotta cheese

1 cup grated Parmesan cheese

1 In a large saucepan over low heat, melt the butter. Increase the heat to medium-high and stir in the onion. Sauté, stirring occasionally, for about 4 minutes.

2 Add the garlic and cook for about 1 more minute. Stir in the all-purpose flour and salt to form a thick paste. Slowly stir in the vegetable broth and milk. Bring to a boil and simmer for 90 seconds to allow the sauce to thicken, then remove from the heat.

3 Stir in 2 cups of the mozzarella cheese along with the basil, oregano, and black pepper. Stir until the cheese is melted and creamy.

4 In a medium bowl, combine the drained spinach, artichoke hearts, and sun-dried tomatoes.

5 Scoop a spoonful of the sauce into the bottom of a 6- to 8-quart (5.5- to 7.5-liter) oval slow cooker. Use the back of the spoon to spread the sauce across the bottom of the slow cooker.

6 Place 2 lasagna pasta sheets parallel in the bottom of the slow cooker. Break a third pasta sheet in half and place at the ends of the oval. (The pasta sheets will expand as they cook.) Top with a third of the ricotta, followed by a third of the spinach mixture and a quarter of the cheese sauce. Repeat two more times to create three layers.

7 Top with the remaining 3 pasta sheets, and sprinkle the remaining mozzarella cheese and Parmesan cheese over the top.

8 Cover and cook on low for 4 to 6 hours.

9 Cut into 8 slices and serve hot. Store in the refrigerator for up to 4 days.

Boston Baked Beans

Sweet and salty navy beans are cooked low and slow in this classic bean dish. Molasses and brown sugar provide the signature sweetness that makes this recipe a family favorite.

YIELD	SERVING SIZE	PREP TIME	COOK TIME
8 CUPS	**1 CUP**	**10 MINUTES, PLUS 8 HOURS SOAK TIME**	**8 TO 10 HOURS**

3 cups dry navy beans, sorted to remove any debris or damaged beans

12 cups water

1 medium yellow onion, diced

1 large red bell pepper, ribs and seeds removed, and diced

¼ cup molasses

1 cup brown sugar (light or dark), firmly packed

2½ cups ketchup

2 tbsp Worcestershire sauce

1 tsp salt

1 tsp garlic powder

1 tsp chili powder

½ tsp ground mustard

½ tsp freshly ground black pepper

1 In a large bowl, cover the navy beans with water and set aside to soak for 8 hours or overnight.

2 Drain the beans and transfer to a 6- to 8-quart (5.5- to 7.5-liter) slow cooker.

3 Stir in the onion, bell pepper, molasses, brown sugar, ketchup, Worcestershire sauce, salt, garlic powder, chili powder, ground mustard, and black pepper.

4 Cover and cook on low for 8 to 10 hours.

5 Serve warm. Store in the refrigerator for up to 4 days.

VARIATION: For a smoky pork flavor, add 1 pound (450g) cooked and crumbled bacon just before serving.

By the Way

There's a debate in the culinary world about whether soaking beans is even necessary. Soaking shortens the beans' cook time, but it might not really do much more than that. Some varieties, however, are quite hard and do benefit from soaking. Without soaking, varieties like navy beans may take 14 to 16 hours or more to cook in the slow cooker.

CHAPTER 11

Breads

You can create delightful breads, rolls, and more in your slow cooker. And one of the best things about using your slow cooker for making breads is that no rising time is required! Some of the amazing recipes featured in this chapter include a hearty Rosemary Focaccia Bread with Sea Salt, classic Cornbread, and a sweet tooth-satisfying Banana Bread.

Dinner Rolls

These soft, pull-apart dinner rolls are perfect for buttering
and serving alongside all kinds of dinners.

YIELD	SERVING SIZE	PREP TIME	COOK TIME
12 ROLLS	**1 ROLL**	**5 MINUTES**	**2 TO 3 HOURS**

1 cup warm reduced fat (2%) milk

2 tbsp instant dry yeast

1 tbsp sugar

1 tsp salt

3 tbsp butter, softened

1 large egg

2½ cups all-purpose flour, plus extra to prevent the dough from sticking

1 Line a 6- to 8-quart (5.5- to 7.5-liter) slow cooker with parchment paper.

2 In a large bowl, combine the warm milk, instant dry yeast, sugar, and salt.

3 Add the butter, egg, and 2½ cups all-purpose flour to the milk and yeast mixture. Using an electric mixer fitted with a dough hook on medium speed, mix until the dough pulls away from the sides of the bowl, adding additional flour as needed to prevent the dough from sticking to the sides of the bowl.

4 Divide the dough into 12 equal-sized pieces, roll the pieces into balls, and then place them in the bottom of the prepared slow cooker so they're touching.

5 Cover and cook on high for 2 to 3 hours.

6 Remove the rolls from the slow cooker and serve warm, or transfer to a wire rack to cool. Once cooled, store in an airtight container or storage bag for up to 3 days.

VARIATION: For shiny, buttery rolls, brush the tops of the cooked rolls with 2 tablespoons melted butter after removing them from the slow cooker.

By the Way

The slow heating process of the slow cooker builds the rising time into the cooking time. By the time the slow cooker reaches maximum temperature (200°F; 90°C), the yeast has had time to work and the dough has begun to rise and cook.

Crusty Loaf Bread

The moisture of the slow cooker creates an easy and versatile, peasant-style loaf bread with a chewy crust and a soft interior. Shape it however you like, from a baguette to a round loaf.

YIELD	SERVING SIZE	PREP TIME	COOK TIME
1 LOAF	**1 SLICE**	**5 MINUTES**	**2 TO 3 HOURS**

1½ tsp instant dry yeast

1½ tsp salt

1 cup lukewarm water

2 cups all-purpose flour, plus extra to prevent the dough from sticking

1 Combine the instant dry yeast, salt, water, and 2 cups of flour in a large bowl. Use an electric mixer on medium speed to knead until the mixture forms a dough ball, adding more flour as needed to prevent the dough from sticking to the sides of the bowl.

2 Remove the dough from the bowl and use your hands to mold it into the desired loaf shape. Place the loaf in a 6- to 8-quart (5.5- to 7.5-liter) slow cooker.

3 Cover and cook on high for 2 to 3 hours or until the loaf sounds hollow when thumped.

4 Immediately remove the bread from the slow cooker and transfer to a wire rack to cool completely. Once sliced, store in an airtight container or airtight storage bag for up to 1 day.

VARIATIONS: For **Crusty Herb Bread,** knead the dried herbs into the dough in step 1. Try 1 teaspoon dried rosemary, basil, or other herb of your choice, or a combination equaling 1 teaspoon. For **Garlic Loaf,** add 2 minced garlic cloves to the dough.

By the Way

Slicing the tops of bread loaves is traditionally done to prevent the loaves from cracking during baking. The slow cooking method doesn't require slicing, but you can still do this for aesthetic purposes. Use a sharp knife to slash a few parallel ¼-inch-deep (.5cm) slices into the top of the dough before cooking.

Pumpkin Bread

This favorite quick bread is flavored with pumpkin and spiced
with the classic spice combination of cinnamon, nutmeg,
cloves, and just a pinch of ginger.

YIELD	SERVING SIZE	PREP TIME	COOK TIME
2 MINI LOAVES OR 1 REGULAR LOAF	**1 SLICE**	**5 MINUTES**	**2 TO 3 HOURS**

1 cup pumpkin purée

2 large eggs

½ cup applesauce

⅓ cup water

1½ cups sugar

1¾ cups all-purpose flour

1 tsp baking soda

¾ tsp salt

½ tsp ground cinnamon

½ tsp ground nutmeg

¼ tsp ground cloves

⅛ tsp ground ginger

1 Lightly coat 2 mini (4.5×2.75×1.25-inch [11.5×7×3cm]) loaf pans or 1 regular (9×5×3-inch [23×12.5×7.5cm]) loaf pan with nonstick cooking spray. Be sure the pan(s) fit into a 6- to 8-quart (5.5- to 7.5-liter) slow cooker.

2 In a large bowl, combine the pumpkin purée, eggs, applesauce, water, sugar, flour, baking soda, salt, cinnamon, nutmeg, cloves, and ginger. Mix until smooth.

3 Pour the batter into the prepared loaf pan(s) and set the pan(s) in the slow cooker.

4 Cover and cook on high for 2 to 3 hours or until the center of the bread is set.

5 Transfer the pan(s) to a wire rack to cool before removing the bread from the pan(s). Once completely cooled, store in an airtight container or storage bag for up to 4 days.

VARIATION: For **Chocolate-Chip Pumpkin Bread,** add ½ cup mini chocolate chips to the batter.

TIP: If you don't have a loaf pan that can fit into your slow cooker, you can cook this bread in a stoneware insert lined with an aluminum foil barrier and parchment paper. Doubling the recipe provides enough batter to yield a nice loaf of bread when cooked in a 6- to 8-quart (5.5- to 7.5-liter) slow cooker.

Cornbread

This sweet, slow-cooked cornbread is incredibly moist. Sweetened with a little sugar and loaded with cornmeal, the result is a bright yellow cornbread that's perfect when paired with soups and stews, as well as many other dishes.

YIELD	SERVING SIZE	PREP TIME	COOK TIME
10 SLICES	**1 SLICE**	**5 MINUTES**	**2 TO 3 HOURS**

½ cup butter, melted

⅔ cup sugar

2 large eggs

1 cup buttermilk

1 cup yellow cornmeal

1 cup all-purpose flour

½ tsp baking soda

½ tsp salt

1 Line a 6- to 8-quart (5.5- to 7.5-liter) slow cooker with an aluminum foil barrier and then line with parchment paper.

2 In a large bowl, whisk together the melted butter, sugar, eggs, and buttermilk until well combined.

3 Stir in the cornmeal, all-purpose flour, baking soda, and salt. Continue stirring until smooth. Pour the batter into the prepared slow cooker.

4 Cover and cook on high for 2 to 3 hours or until the center of the cornbread is set.

5 Transfer the cornbread to a wire rack to cool. Once completely cooled, store in an airtight container or storage bag for up to 3 days.

VARIATION: For **Chunky-Style Cornbread,** add 1 cup frozen corn kernels that have been thawed and drained to the batter in step 3.

By the Way

Traditional cornbread made in the southern United States is made without any sugar, while most non-southerners are accustomed to a sweetened version.

Rosemary Focaccia Bread with Sea Salt

Fluffy focaccia is sprinkled with sea salt and rosemary in this olive oil–glazed Italian bread. The slow cooker yields a crispy bottom crust and a steamed top that's perfectly delicious.

YIELD	SERVING SIZE	PREP TIME	COOK TIME
10 PIECES	**1 PIECE**	**5 MINUTES**	**2 HOURS**

1 cup warm water

1½ tsp salt

1½ tsp instant dry yeast

1½ tsp sugar

2 tbsp olive oil, divided

2 cups all-purpose flour, plus extra to prevent the dough from sticking

1 tsp dried rosemary

¼ tsp sea salt

1 In a large bowl, combine the warm water, salt, instant dry yeast, sugar, 1 tablespoon olive oil, and 2 cups flour.

2 Using an electric mixer fitted with a dough hook on medium speed, knead the dough until it pulls away from the sides of the bowl and forms a large ball, adding additional flour as needed to prevent the dough from sticking to the sides of the bowl.

3 Turn the dough out onto a lightly floured surface. Roll to ½ inch (1.25cm) thick.

4 Using your hands, stretch the dough to fit the shape of the bottom of a 6- to 8-quart (5.5- to 7.5-liter) slow cooker. Place the dough in the slow cooker.

5 Drizzle the remaining 1 tablespoon of olive oil over the dough, and then sprinkle the rosemary and sea salt over the top. Use your fingertips to create indentations all over the surface of the dough.

6 Cover and cook on high for 2 hours.

7 Transfer the focaccia to a wire rack to cool. Once cooled and sliced, store in an airtight container or storage bag for up to 1 day.

VARIATION: For **Olive Focaccia Bread,** add ½ cup sliced olives to the top of the dough in step 5. When creating indentations in the dough, gently press the olives into the loaf.

By the Way

Creating indentations in the dough gives the finished focaccia its traditional dotted look and creates small wells for the olive oil to puddle in, keeping the bread moist.

Light Rye Bread

Caraway plays the starring role in this delicious light rye. And you can create a dark rye by adding just a few simple ingredients. Nothing beats a tuna on rye, and Reuben sandwiches wouldn't be the same without the rye!

YIELD	SERVING SIZE	PREP TIME	COOK TIME
1 LOAF	**1 SLICE**	**5 MINUTES**	**2 TO 3 HOURS**

1½ tsp instant dry yeast

2 cups water

2 tsp caraway seeds

1 tsp salt

1 cup rye flour

1 to 1½ cups all-purpose flour

1 In a large bowl, combine the instant dry yeast, water, caraway seeds, salt, rye flour, and 1 cup all-purpose flour.

2 Using an electric mixer fitted with a dough hook on medium speed, knead the dough until it pulls away from the sides of the bowl and forms a large ball, adding additional all-purpose flour as needed to prevent the dough from sticking to the sides of the bowl.

3 Shape the dough into a ball and place it in the bottom of a 6- to 8-quart (5.5- to 7.5-liter) slow cooker.

4 Cover and cook on high for 2 to 3 hours.

5 Transfer the loaf to a wire rack to cool. Once cooled and sliced, store in an airtight container or storage bag for up to 1 day.

VARIATION: For **Dark Rye Bread,** add 3 tablespoons dark brown sugar, 2 tablespoons molasses, and 1 tablespoon cocoa powder with the flours. (Note that you probably won't need to add as much all-purpose flour to the dough.)

By the Way

In the United States, rye bread is often just used for sandwiches. Don't limit your rye to just sandwiches, though. You can make it into a delicious toast, or just enjoy the distinct flavors of caraway and rye served plain as a side.

Banana Bread

Extra-ripe banana imparts a rich banana flavor to this sweet, moist bread, while chopped walnuts add a pleasant crunch.

YIELD	SERVING SIZE	PREP TIME	COOK TIME
2 MINI LOAVES OR 1 REGULAR LOAF	**1 SLICE**	**5 MINUTES**	**2 TO 3 HOURS**

¼ cup butter, melted

½ cup sugar

1 large egg

½ tsp pure vanilla extract

¾ cup all-purpose flour

½ tsp baking soda

¼ tsp salt

¼ cup sour cream

¼ cup chopped walnuts

1 very ripe medium banana, peeled and mashed

By the Way

Bananas don't "go bad" as much as they change stages of ripeness. Bananas start out green and turn yellow as they ripen. Black spots start to appear after a few days, signifying a change in the bananas' ripeness—and sweetness. Spotted bananas are sweeter. Bananas that have completely black skins have an intense flavor and are best for use in breads, puddings, and pies.

1 Lightly coat 2 mini (4.5×2.75×1.25-inch [11.5×7×3cm]) loaf pans or 1 regular (9×5×3-inch [23×12.5×7.5cm]) loaf pan with nonstick cooking spray. Be sure the pan(s) fit into a 6- to 8-quart (5.5- to 7.5-liter) slow cooker.

2 In a large bowl, combine the melted butter, sugar, egg, and vanilla extract. Mix until the egg is well incorporated.

3 Stir in the flour, baking soda, and salt and continue stirring until smooth.

4 Fold in the sour cream, chopped walnuts, and mashed banana.

5 Pour the batter into the prepared pan(s) and set the pan(s) in the slow cooker.

6 Cover and cook on high for 2 to 3 hours or until the center of the bread is set.

7 Transfer the pan(s) to a wire rack to cool before removing the bread from the pan(s). Once completely cooled, store in an airtight container or storage bag for up to 4 days.

TIP: You can easily double this recipe and cook the bread in a 6- to 8-quart (5.5- to 7.5-liter) slow cooker lined with parchment paper.

CHAPTER 12

Sweets

Perhaps the most pleasant surprise of the slow cooker
is its ability to produce some amazing desserts with
absolute ease. What's more, the cook times are generally
short, so you can get your dessert going first and have
it hot and ready when dinner is over. This is particularly
useful when hosting guests or dinner parties, and
it frees you up to enjoy your company instead
of being stuck in the kitchen.

Apple Crumble

These cinnamon and sugar–coated apples are cooked until delicate and caramelized, and then topped with a brown sugar and oat crumble.

YIELD	SERVING SIZE	PREP TIME	COOK TIME
8 CUPS	**1 CUP**	**15 MINUTES**	**3 TO 4 HOURS**

10 medium apples (Gala, Golden Delicious, Granny Smith, or Honeycrisp varieties suggested), peeled, cored, and sliced

1 cup sugar

1 tsp cornstarch

1 tsp ground cinnamon

1 cup quick oats

1 cup all-purpose flour

1 cup brown sugar, firmly packed

¼ tsp baking powder

¼ tsp baking soda

½ cup butter

1 Add the apples to a 6- to 8-quart (5.5- to 7.5-liter) slow cooker. Sprinkle in the sugar, cornstarch, and cinnamon. Gently toss to combine.

2 In a medium bowl, combine the oats, flour, brown sugar, baking powder, and baking soda.

3 Using a pastry cutter or two butter knives, cut the butter into the flour mixture until it resembles cornmeal. Sprinkle the oat mixture over the apples in the slow cooker.

4 Cover and cook on high for 3 to 4 hours or until the apples are tender.

5 Serve hot. Store the cooled crumble in the refrigerator for up to 4 days.

VARIATION: For **Apple-Blueberry Crumble,** replace 2 apples with 2 cups fresh or frozen blueberries (thawed, if frozen).

TIP: Be sure to use an apple variety that is good for all-around cooking. Some varieties like McIntosh break down more easily and are great for applesauce, but they don't hold their shape well for recipes like crumbles. Other varieties, like Red Delicious, are best eaten out of hand.

Apple Dumplings

Soft and warm sugar-and-spice apples are wrapped in a sweet
pastry dough and drizzled with a cinnamon buttermilk syrup
for an updated version of this old-fashioned favorite.

YIELD	SERVING SIZE	PREP TIME	COOK TIME
4 DUMPLINGS	**1 DUMPLING**	**20 MINUTES**	**3 TO 4 HOURS**

2 cups all-purpose flour

¾ cup confectioners'
sugar

1 tbsp baking powder

1 tsp salt

1¼ cups butter, divided

½ cup reduced fat (2%)
milk

¼ cup brown sugar,
firmly packed

1½ tsp ground
cinnamon, divided

½ tsp ground nutmeg

4 medium Granny Smith
apples, peeled and
cored

1 cup sugar

1 cup buttermilk

1 tbsp pure vanilla
extract

½ tsp baking soda

1 In a large bowl, combine the flour, confectioners' sugar, baking powder, and salt.

2 Using a pastry cutter or 2 butter knives, cut ½ cup butter into the flour mixture until it resembles cornmeal.

3 Pour in the milk. Using your hands, knead the mixture into a ball of dough. Turn the dough out onto a lightly floured surface. Using a rolling pin, roll the dough into a ¼-inch-thick (.5-centimeter-thick) square and then cut into 4 squares.

4 In a small bowl, combine the brown sugar, ¼ cup butter, 1 teaspoon cinnamon, and the nutmeg.

5 Place 1 apple on each dough square. Divide the brown sugar mixture among the apples, filling the hollowed-out cores.

6 Gently pull the dough up and around the apples, wrapping each apple entirely in the dough and then pinching the seams together.

7 Place the wrapped apples in a 6- to 8-quart (5.5- to 7.5-liter) slow cooker.

8 Cover and cook on high for 3 to 4 hours.

9 While the apples are cooking, in a large saucepan over medium heat, melt the remaining ½ cup butter. Stir in the sugar, buttermilk, vanilla extract, and remaining ½ teaspoon cinnamon. Increase the heat to high, bring to a boil and then boil for 90 seconds. Remove from the heat and stir in the baking soda until the foam dissipates.

10 Drizzle the syrup over the dumplings and serve hot. Store in the refrigerator for up 4 days.

By the Way

Don't substitute puff pastry for the dough made in this recipe. Puff pastry requires a blast of heat in order to puff.

Chocolate Mud Cake

Gooey, *rich*, and *decadent* hardly begin to describe this magnificent chocolate dessert. Serve with a scoop of vanilla ice cream for an indulgent hot and cold dessert.

YIELD	SERVING SIZE	PREP TIME	COOK TIME
6 CUPS	**¾ CUP**	**5 MINUTES**	**2 TO 3 HOURS**

1 cup all-purpose flour

1 cup sugar

¾ cup unsweetened cocoa powder, divided

1 tsp baking soda

½ tsp baking powder

½ tsp salt

½ cup buttermilk

½ cup water

2 tbsp vegetable oil

1 tsp pure vanilla extract

1 cup milk or semisweet chocolate chips

¾ cup brown sugar, firmly packed

1½ cups hot water

1 In a large bowl, combine the flour, sugar, ½ cup cocoa powder, baking soda, baking powder, salt, buttermilk, water, vegetable oil, and vanilla extract. Pour the batter into a 6- to 8-quart (5.5- to 7.5-liter) slow cooker.

2 Sprinkle the chocolate chips, brown sugar, and remaining ¼ cup cocoa powder over the top of the cake batter.

3 Pour the hot water over the cake. (Do not stir.)

4 Cover and cook on high for 2 to 3 hours.

5 Serve warm. Store in the refrigerator for up to 4 days.

By the Way

This recipe produces a very gooey cake, but as the cake cools, it will begin to firm up. While you can eat this cake cooled, it's best served warm and gooey.

Vanilla Poached Pears

Sweet, juicy pears are cooked to tender perfection in a tart and sweet vanilla-orange syrup. Cinnamon adds a warm and inviting flavor to this fantastic fruit dessert.

YIELD	SERVING SIZE	PREP TIME	COOK TIME
6 PEARS	**1 PEAR**	**10 MINUTES**	**2 HOURS**

6 medium pears (any variety), peeled

1½ cups orange juice

½ cup brown sugar (light or dark), firmly packed

¼ cup sugar

1 tbsp pure vanilla extract

1 tsp ground cinnamon

1 Core the pears from the bottoms, leaving the stems intact. Place the cored pears on their sides in a 6- to 8-quart (5.5- to 7.5-liter) slow cooker.

2 In a medium bowl, whisk together the orange juice, brown sugar, sugar, vanilla extract, and cinnamon. Pour the syrup over the pears.

3 Cover and cook on high for 1 hour. After 1 hour, flip the pears over and cook on high for 1 more hour or until the pears are soft.

4 Transfer to serving bowls and drizzle the juices over the pears. Serve warm. Store in the refrigerator for up to 4 days.

By the Way

Turning the pears on their sides allows them to soak in the flavors of the syrup. Flipping the pears halfway through the cook time ensures they will be fully poached.

Lemon Pound Cake

The subtle citrus flavor of lemon brightens this sweet and dense cake that is delicious served as a treat or as a dessert. The slow cooker keeps the cake extra moist for a perfect pound cake.

YIELD	SERVING SIZE	PREP TIME	COOK TIME
12 SLICES	**1 SLICE**	**5 MINUTES**	**3 HOURS**

3 cups all-purpose flour

3 cups sugar

½ tsp salt

¼ tsp baking soda

1 cup butter, softened

6 large eggs

1 cup buttermilk

1 tsp pure lemon extract

1 tsp pure vanilla extract

2 tbsp lemon zest

1 Line a 6- to 8-quart (5.5- to 7.5-liter) slow cooker with an aluminum foil barrier and then parchment paper.

2 In a large bowl, combine the flour, sugar, salt, and baking soda.

3 Using an electric mixer on medium speed, whip the butter into the flour mixture. Mix in the eggs, buttermilk, lemon extract, vanilla extract, and lemon zest until smooth. Pour the batter into the prepared slow cooker.

4 Cover and cook on high for 3 hours or until the cake is set in the middle.

5 Transfer the cake to a wire rack to cool before slicing. Store in the refrigerator for up to 4 days.

VARIATION: For **Orange Pound Cake,** use orange extract in place of lemon extract and orange zest in place of lemon zest. You also can dust the top of the cooled cake with confectioners' sugar before slicing.

TIP: Slicing a slow cooker cake can be a bit tricky, particularly if you're using an oval-shaped cooker. For presentation purposes, square off the cake first and then cut as you would a traditional cake. Or simply enjoy the rounded sides.

Peach Cobbler

Peaches sweetened with sugar and brightened with lemon
serve as the base for this tasty cobbler. A sweet biscuit dough
is heaped on top to provide the ultimate cobbler topping.

YIELD	SERVING SIZE	PREP TIME	COOK TIME
8 CUPS	**1 CUP**	**30 MINUTES**	**3 TO 4 HOURS**

8 medium fresh peaches,
  pitted, peeled, and sliced

⅓ cup sugar

Zest of 1 medium lemon

Juice of 1 medium lemon

2 tsp cornstarch

½ tsp pure vanilla extract

2 cups all-purpose flour

1 tsp salt

1 tbsp baking powder

¾ cup confectioners' sugar

½ cup butter

1 cup half & half

1 Add the peaches, sugar, lemon zest, lemon juice, cornstarch, and vanilla extract to a 6- to 8-quart (5.5- to 7.5-liter) slow cooker. Toss to combine.

2 In a large bowl, combine the flour, salt, baking powder, and confectioners' sugar. Using a pastry cutter or two butter knives, cut the butter into the flour mixture until it resembles cornmeal.

3 Slowly stir the half & half into the butter mixture to form a thick batter. Spoon the batter over the peaches in large heaps.

4 Cover and cook on high for 3 to 4 hours or until the dough is cooked through.

5 Serve hot. Store in the refrigerator for up to 4 days.

VARIATION: For **Berry Cobbler,** use a mixture of 3 cups fresh berries instead of peaches. For **Apple Cobbler,** use 8 medium apples that have been peeled, cored, and sliced.

TIP: If fresh peaches are not in season, you can substitute 4 (15oz [420g]) cans of packed-in-water peaches (not packed in syrup) that have been drained.

Mile-High Chocolate Fudge Brownies

These brownies are thick and gooey, with a fudge-like texture that's worthy of being devoured.

YIELD	SERVING SIZE	PREP TIME	COOK TIME
12 SLICES	**1 SLICE**	**5 MINUTES**	**3 TO 4 HOURS**

1 cup butter, melted

2¼ cups sugar

4 large eggs

1¼ cups unsweetened cocoa powder

1 tsp salt

1 tsp baking powder

1 tbsp pure vanilla extract

1½ cups all-purpose flour

1 cup milk chocolate chips

1 Line a 6- to 8-quart (5.5- to 7.5-liter) slow cooker with an aluminum foil barrier and then parchment paper.

2 In a large bowl, use a large rubber spatula to combine the butter and sugar.

3 Using an electric mixer on medium speed, mix in the eggs and then reduce the mixer speed to low and mix in cocoa powder, salt, baking powder, and vanilla extract.

4 Using the spatula, stir in the flour and chocolate chips. Pour the batter into the slow cooker.

5 Cover and cook on high for 3 to 4 hours or until the center of the brownies is firm.

6 Transfer the brownies to a wire rack to cool before slicing. Store in the refrigerator for up to 4 days.

TIP: It can be difficult to tell when brownies, breads, and other desserts are finished in the slow cooker because the center often remains shiny and appears to be uncooked. The best way to test for doneness is to tug on the parchment liner to see if the middle jiggles. If it jiggles, the center is still undercooked.

Almond Poppy Seed Cake

The sweet flavors of almond and poppy seeds are combined in a traditional white cake to create a lusciously sweet and nutty dessert.

YIELD	SERVING SIZE	PREP TIME	COOK TIME
12 SLICES	**1 SLICE**	**30 MINUTES**	**3 TO 4 HOURS**

2½ cups all-purpose flour

2 cups sugar

1 tsp baking powder

½ tsp baking soda

1⅓ cups buttermilk

½ cup butter, melted

1 tsp pure almond extract

2 large eggs

1 tbsp poppy seeds

1 Line a 6- to 8-quart (5.5- to 7.5-liter) slow cooker with an aluminum foil barrier and then parchment paper.

2 In a large bowl, combine the flour, sugar, baking powder, and baking soda. Stir until well combined.

3 Add the buttermilk, melted butter, almond extract, eggs, and poppy seeds. Whisk until smooth. Pour the batter into the prepared slow cooker.

4 Cover and cook on high for 3 to 4 hours or until the center of the cake is set.

5 Transfer the cake to a wire rack to cool before slicing. Store in the refrigerator for up to 4 days.

VARIATION: For **Lemon Poppy Seed Cake,** replace the almond extract with lemon extract. For a **Simple White Cake,** replace the almond extract with vanilla extract and omit the poppy seeds.

TIP: This cake is sweet enough that it doesn't require any frosting, but a simple glaze can add a nice touch. In a small bowl, whisk together 1½ cups confectioners' sugar with 2 tablespoons milk. Add more milk, as needed, to achieve the consistency you want. Allow the cake to cool completely before pouring the glaze over the top.

Peanut Butter Fudge Cake

A soft and gooey peanut butter cake sits atop a hot fudge layer of chocolate goodness in this indulgent dessert that is perfect for lovers of chocolate and peanut butter.

YIELD	SERVING SIZE	PREP TIME	COOK TIME
6 CUPS	**¾ CUP**	**5 MINUTES**	**2 TO 3 HOURS**

1 cup all-purpose flour

1 cup sugar

½ cup creamy peanut butter

1 tsp baking soda

½ tsp baking powder

½ tsp salt

½ cup buttermilk

½ cup water

2 tbsp vegetable oil

1 tsp pure vanilla extract

1 cup milk or semisweet chocolate chips

½ cup brown sugar (light or dark), firmly packed

¼ cup unsweetened cocoa powder

1¼ cups boiling water

1 In a large bowl, combine the flour, sugar, peanut butter, baking soda, baking powder, salt, buttermilk, water, vegetable oil, and vanilla extract. Pour the mixture into a 6- to 8-quart (5.5- to 7.5-liter) slow cooker.

2 Sprinkle the chocolate chips, brown sugar, and cocoa powder over the top of the batter.

3 Pour the boiling water over the cake batter. (Do not stir.)

4 Cover and cook on high for 2 to 3 hours.

5 Serve warm. Store in the refrigerator for up to 4 days.

By the Way

This cake is assembled with the peanut butter cake on bottom and the fudge layer on top, but the layers reverse during cooking!

S'mores Brownies

The traditional elements of campfire s'mores are layered into a rich fudge brownie topped with puffy marshmallows.

YIELD	SERVING SIZE	PREP TIME	COOK TIME
12 SLICES	**1 SLICE**	**10 MINUTES**	**3 TO 4 HOURS**

½ cup butter, melted

1 cup sugar

2 large eggs

½ cup unsweetened cocoa powder

½ tsp salt

½ tsp baking powder

1½ tsp pure vanilla extract

¾ cup all-purpose flour

4 (5x2½-inch [12x5.6cm]) graham cracker sheets

3 (1.5oz [40g]) milk chocolate candy bars

3 cups mini marshmallows, divided

1 Line a 6- to 8-quart (5.5- to 7.5-liter) slow cooker with an aluminum foil barrier and then parchment paper.

2 In a large bowl, use a large rubber spatula to combine the butter and sugar.

3 Using an electric mixer on medium speed, mix in the eggs and then reduce the mixer speed to low and mix in the cocoa powder, salt, baking powder, and vanilla extract. Use the spatula to stir in the flour.

4 Pour half of the batter into the slow cooker. Create a single layer of graham crackers on top of the batter, breaking the crackers to fit, if needed. Break the chocolate bars into pieces and scatter the pieces in a single layer on top of the graham crackers.

5 Stir 1 cup mini marshmallows into the remaining brownie batter and pour the mixture over the top of the chocolate bars.

6 Cover and cook on high for 3 to 4 hours or until the middle of the brownies is firm.

7 Sprinkle the remaining 2 cups of mini marshmallows over the cooked brownies.

8 Transfer the brownies to a wire rack to cool before slicing. Store in the refrigerator for up to 4 days.

By the Way

The marshmallows are added in two spots because they liquefy when heated. The first cup melts and adds sweetness to the top brownie layer, and the remaining 2 cups stay mostly intact on top.

Strawberry Swirl Cheesecakes

Making a silky cheesecake has never been easier than these individual-sized cakes that are complete with graham cracker crusts and a sweet strawberry swirl.

YIELD	SERVING SIZE	PREP TIME	COOK TIME
5 CHEESECAKES	**1 CHEESECAKE**	**10 MINUTES**	**2 HOURS**

1 cup crushed graham crackers

3 tbsp butter, melted

2 (8oz [225g]) packages cream cheese, softened

¾ cup sugar

⅓ cup reduced fat (2%) milk

2 large eggs

½ cup sour cream

1½ tsp pure vanilla extract

2 tbsp all-purpose flour

5 tsp strawberry jam

1 In a small bowl, combine the graham cracker crumbs and butter. Evenly divide the crust mixture among 5 (8oz [225ml]) wide-mouth jars, and firmly press down on the mixture to form crusts.

2 In a large bowl, use an electric mixer on medium speed to beat the cream cheese, sugar, milk, eggs, sour cream, vanilla extract, and flour until smooth.

3 Divide the batter among the jars, filling them to just below the rim. (The cheesecakes will puff up slightly as they cook.)

4 Place 1 teaspoon strawberry jam on top of each cake and then use a toothpick or butter knife to swirl the jam gently into the top of the batter.

5 Place the jars in a 6- to 8-quart (5.5- to 7.5-liter) slow cooker. Carefully pour water around the jars to cover the bottom of the slow cooker with 1 inch (2.5cm) of water.

6 Cover and cook on high for 2 hours.

7 Carefully transfer the jars to a wire rack to cool. Cover and store in the refrigerator for up to 4 days.

VARIATION: You can use different flavors of jam to create a mix-and-match variety.

By the Way

This recipe shows how the slow cooker can work as a miniature oven, baking individual cakes in their own containers. Any oven-safe dish that fits into your slow cooker, including ramekins, springform pans, or even pie plates, will work.

Salted Caramel Rice Pudding

Creamy rice pudding is swirled with a homemade salted caramel sauce for a decadently sweet version of classic rice pudding.

YIELD	SERVING SIZE	PREP TIME	COOK TIME
6 CUPS	**1 CUP**	**15 MINUTES**	**2½ TO 3½ HOURS**

¾ cup Arborio rice

3 cups reduced fat (2%) milk

1½ cups sugar, divided

1¼ tsp salt, divided

1 large egg

6 tbsp butter, diced

½ cup heavy cream

1 Add the rice to a 3- or 4-quart (3- to 4-liter) slow cooker.

2 In a medium bowl, whisk together the milk, ½ cup sugar, ¼ teaspoon salt, and the egg. Pour the mixture over the rice.

3 Cover and cook on high for 2½ to 3½ hours or until the rice is cooked through and most of liquids are absorbed, leaving a creamy sauce.

4 While the rice is cooking, combine the butter and remaining 1 cup sugar in a small saucepan over medium heat. Cook, stirring constantly, for 3 to 5 minutes or until the butter and sugar are melted and turn a golden color.

5 Slowly pour in the heavy cream, bring to a boil, and simmer for 2 minutes, then remove from the heat and stir in the remaining 1 teaspoon salt.

6 Stir half of the salted caramel sauce into the cooked rice pudding.

7 Drizzle the remaining caramel sauce over the top and serve hot. Store in the refrigerator for up to 4 days.

TIP: If you don't have time to make your own caramel sauce, you can use a jar of caramel ice cream topping instead.

By the Way

Traditional rice pudding is made with vanilla extract, butter, raisins, and either long- or short-grain white rice. Arborio rice holds up better in slow cooking and produces a hearty rice pudding. It also has a natural creaminess, thanks to its additional starch that enriches the pudding's creamy texture.

White Chocolate Bread Pudding

Buttery croissants are soaked in a vanilla custard and sprinkled with chunks of white chocolate in this ultra decadent bread pudding.

YIELD	SERVING SIZE	PREP TIME	COOK TIME
8 SLICES	**1 SLICE**	**5 MINUTES**	**4 TO 6 HOURS**

6 large croissants, torn into bite-sized pieces

2 cups white chocolate chips

8 large eggs

2 cups reduced fat (2%) milk

2 cups heavy cream

⅔ cup sugar

1 tsp pure vanilla extract

1 Line a 6- to 8-quart (5.5- to 7.5-liter) slow cooker with parchment paper.

2 Place the bread pieces in the slow cooker. Sprinkle the white chocolate chips over the bread pieces.

3 In a large bowl, use a whisk to beat the eggs until well combined. Whisk in the milk, heavy cream, sugar, and vanilla extract. Pour the mixture over the bread.

4 Cover and cook on low for 6 hours or on high for 4 hours.

5 Cut the pudding into 8 slices and serve warm. Store in the refrigerator for up to 4 days.

VARIATION: For **Milk Chocolate Bread Pudding,** use milk chocolate chips in place of the white chocolate chips and add ⅓ cup unsweetened cocoa powder with the sugar.

By the Way

The kind of bread you use in a bread pudding affects the end result in both taste and texture. You can use French bread, as well as challah, brioche, and even sourdough.

Caramelitas

Featuring layers of gooey caramel and melted chocolate sandwiched between soft oatmeal-cookie layers, these dessert bars will be a fast favorite at any party.

YIELD	SERVING SIZE	PREP TIME	COOK TIME
12 BARS	**1 BAR**	**5 MINUTES**	**2 TO 3 HOURS**

2 cups all-purpose flour

2 cups quick oats

1½ cups brown sugar, firmly packed

1 tsp baking soda

½ tsp salt

1 cup butter, melted

2 cups semisweet chocolate chips

1 (12oz [340g]) jar caramel ice cream topping

1 Line a 6- to 8-quart (5.5- to 7.5-liter) slow cooker with parchment paper.

2 In a large bowl, combine the flour, oats, brown sugar, baking soda, and salt.

3 Add the melted butter and stir to form a crumbly oat mixture. Pour half of the mixture into the bottom of the prepared slow cooker. Press down on the mixture to form a smooth crust.

4 Sprinkle the chocolate chips evenly over the crust, pour the caramel ice cream topping over the chocolate chips, and then pour the remaining oat mixture over the caramel. Press down gently to form a smooth top crust.

5 Cover and cook on high for 2 to 3 hours.

6 Carefully lift the parchment paper to transfer the caramelitas to a wire rack to cool before slicing. Store in the refrigerator for up to 4 days.

VARIATION: To add a nutty crunch, sprinkle ½ cup chopped walnuts over the caramel layer.

By the Way

Lining the slow cooker with parchment paper is a key step because it enables you to easily remove the bars from the slow cooker. While hot, the bars will be unstable, but they'll set as they cool. These bars are delicious when eaten hot with a spoon, but they can't be cut into bars until after they're completely cooled.

Glossary

all-purpose flour Flour that contains only the inner part of the wheat grain. It's suitable for everything from cakes to gravies.

allspice A spice named for its flavor echoes of several spices such as cinnamon, cloves, and nutmeg.

Arborio rice A plump Italian rice often used for risotto.

artichoke heart The center of the artichoke flower, often sold canned or frozen.

arugula A spicy-peppery green that has a sharp, distinctive flavor.

baking powder A dry ingredient used to increase volume and lighten or leaven baked goods.

balsamic vinegar A heavy, dark, sweet vinegar produced primarily in Italy from a specific type of grape and aged in wood barrels.

basil A flavorful, almost sweet, resinous herb delicious with tomatoes and used in many Italian- and Mediterranean-style dishes.

beat To quickly mix substances.

blanch To place a food in boiling water for about 1 minute or less to partially cook and then douse with cool water to halt the cooking.

blend To completely mix something, usually with a blender or food processor, slower than beating.

boil To heat a liquid to the point where water is forced to turn into steam, causing the liquid to bubble.

bouillon Dried essence of stock from chicken, beef, vegetables, or other ingredients.

braise To cook with the introduction of a liquid, usually over a period of time.

broil To cook in a dry oven under the overhead high-heat element.

broth *See stock.*

brown To cook in a skillet, turning, until the food's surface is seared and brown in color, to lock in the juices.

brown rice A nutritious whole-grain rice, including the germ, with a pale brown or tan color.

bulgur A wheat kernel that's been steamed, dried, and crushed.

caramelize To cook vegetables or meat in butter or oil over low heat until they soften, sweeten, and develop a caramel color. Also to cook sugar over low heat until it develops a sweet caramel flavor.

caraway A spicy seed used for bread, pork, cheese, and cabbage dishes. It's known to reduce stomach upset.

cardamom An intense, sweet-smelling spice used in baking and coffee and common in Indian cooking.

cayenne A fiery spice made from hot chile peppers, especially the slender, red, very hot cayenne.

chickpea (or garbanzo bean) A roundish, golden bean high in fiber and low in fat, often used as the base ingredient in hummus.

chile (or chili) A term for a number of hot peppers, ranging from the relatively mild ancho to the blisteringly hot habanero.

chili powder A warm, rich seasoning blend that includes chile pepper, cumin, garlic, and oregano.

chive A herb that grows in bunches of long leaves and offers a light onion flavor.

chop To cut into pieces, usually qualified such as "coarsely chopped" or with a size measurement such as "chopped into ½-inch (1.25cm) pieces." "Finely chopped" is much closer to mince.

chutney A thick condiment often served with Indian curries made with fruits and/or vegetables with vinegar, sugar, and spices.

cilantro   A member of the parsley family often used in Mexican dishes. The seed is called coriander in North America; elsewhere, the plant is called coriander.

cinnamon   A rich, aromatic spice commonly used in baking or desserts.

clove   A sweet, strong, almost wintergreen-flavor spice used in baking.

coriander   A rich, warm, spicy seed used in all types of recipes.

cornstarch   A thickener made from the refined starch of a corn kernel's endosperm. Before it's added to a recipe, it's often mixed with a liquid to make a paste and avoid clumps.

cream   To beat a fat such as butter, often with another ingredient such as sugar, to soften and aerate a batter.

cumin   A fiery, smoky-tasting spice popular in Middle Eastern and Indian dishes. It's most often used ground.

curry   Rich, spicy, Indian-style sauces and the dishes prepared with them. Curry powder is the base seasoning.

curry powder   A ground blend of rich and flavorful spices such as hot pepper, nutmeg, cumin, cinnamon, pepper, and turmeric.

custard   A cooked mixture of eggs and milk popular as a base for desserts.

dash   A few drops, usually of a liquid, released by a quick shake.

deglaze   To scrape up bits of meat and seasoning left in a pan or skillet after cooking, usually by adding a liquid such as wine or broth and creating a flavorful stock.

dice   To cut into small cubes about 1/4-inch (6.5mm) square.

Dijon mustard   A hearty, spicy mustard made in the style of the Dijon region of France.

dill   A herb perfect for eggs, salmon, cheese dishes, and vegetables.

dredge   To coat a piece of food on all sides with a dry substance such as flour or cornmeal.

extra-virgin olive oil   See olive oil.

falafel   A Middle Eastern food made of seasoned, ground chickpeas formed into balls, cooked, and often used as a filling in pitas.

fennel   In seed form, a fragrant, licorice-tasting herb. The bulbs have a mild flavor and a celery-like crunch.

flour   Grains ground into a meal. Wheat is perhaps the most common flour, but oats, rye, buckwheat, soybeans, chickpeas, and others are also used.

fold   To combine a dense and a light mixture with a gentle move from the middle of the bowl outward to preserve the mixture's airy nature.

frittata   An egg dish that's cooked slowly, without stirring, in a skillet and then either flipped or finished under the broiler.

fry   See sauté.

garlic   A pungent and flavorful member of the onion family. A garlic bulb contains multiple cloves; each clove, when chopped, yields about 1 teaspoon garlic.

ginger   A flavorful root available fresh or dried and ground that adds a pungent, sweet, and spicy quality to a dish.

Greek yogurt   A strained yogurt that's a good natural source of protein, calcium, and probiotics.

hearts of palm   Firm, elongated, off-white cylinders from the inside of a palm tree stem tip.

herbes de Provence   A seasoning mix of basil, fennel, marjoram, rosemary, sage, and thyme, common in the south of France.

hoisin sauce   A sweet Asian condiment similar to ketchup made with soybeans, sesame, chile peppers, and sugar.

horseradish　A sharp, spicy root. (Use sparingly.)

hummus　A thick, Middle Eastern spread made of puréed chickpeas, lemon juice, olive oil, garlic, and often tahini.

Italian seasoning　A blend of dried herbs, including basil, oregano, rosemary, and thyme.

julienne　A French word meaning "to slice into very thin pieces."

Kalamata olive　Traditionally from Greece, a medium-small, long black olive with a rich, smoky flavor.

Key lime　A very small lime grown primarily in Florida known for its tart taste.

knead　To work dough, often with your hands, to make it pliable. Kneading is fundamental in the process of making yeast breads.

kosher salt　A coarse-grained salt made without any additives or iodine.

lentil　A tiny lens-shape pulse used in European, Middle Eastern, and Indian cuisines.

marinate　To soak a food in a seasoned sauce to impart flavor and make tender, as with meat.

marjoram　A sweet herb similar to oregano popular in Greek, Spanish, and Italian dishes.

mince　To cut into very small pieces, smaller than diced, about ⅛ inch (3.18mm) or smaller.

nutmeg　A sweet, fragrant, musky spice used primarily in baking.

olive　The green or black fruit of the olive tree.

olive oil　A fragrant liquid produced by crushing or pressing olives. Extra-virgin olive oil, the most flavorful and highest quality, is produced from the olives' first pressing; oil is also produced from later pressings.

oregano　A fragrant, slightly astringent herb used often in Greek, Spanish, and Italian dishes.

orzo　A rice-shape pasta used in Greek cooking.

oxidation　The gradual browning of a fruit or vegetable from exposure to air. Minimize oxidation by rubbing cut surfaces with lemon juice.

paella　A Spanish dish of rice, shellfish, onion, meats, rich broth, and herbs.

paprika　A rich, red, warm, earthy spice that lends a rich red color to many dishes.

parsley　A fresh-tasting green leafy herb, often used as a garnish.

pesto　A thick spread or sauce made with pine nuts, fresh basil, garlic, olive oil, and Parmesan cheese.

pilaf　A savory rice dish in which the rice is browned in butter or oil and then cooked in a flavorful liquid such as a broth.

pine nut　A rich (high in fat), flavorful, nut traditionally used in pesto.

poach　To cook a food in simmering liquid such as water, wine, or broth.

polenta　A cornmeal mush that can be eaten hot with butter or cooked until firm and cut into squares.

portobello mushroom　A large, brown, chewy, flavorful mushroom.

purée　To reduce a food to a thick, creamy texture, typically using a blender or food processor.

quinoa　A nutty-flavored seed high in protein and calcium.

reduce　To boil or simmer a broth or sauce to remove some of the water content and yield a more concentrated flavor.

risotto　A creamy Italian rice dish made by browning Arborio rice in butter or oil and slowly adding liquid to cook the rice.

roast　To cook food uncovered in an oven, usually without additional liquid.

rosemary   A pungent, sweet herb used with chicken, pork, fish, and especially lamb.

roux   A mixture of butter or another fat and flour used to thicken sauces and soups.

saffron   A yellow, flavorful spice made from the stamens of crocus flowers.

sage   An herb with a slightly musty, fruity, lemon-rind scent and sunny flavor.

sauté   To pan-cook over lower heat than what's used for frying.

savory   A popular herb with a fresh, woody taste. Savory can also describe the flavor of food.

sear   To quickly brown the exterior of a food, especially meat, over high heat.

sesame oil   An oil made from pressing sesame seeds. It's tasteless if clear and aromatic and flavorful if brown.

shallot   A member of the onion family that grows in a bulb somewhat like garlic but has a milder onion flavor.

short-grain rice   A starchy rice that clumps easily.

simmer   To boil a liquid gently so it barely bubbles.

skillet (also frying pan)   A flat-bottomed metal pan with a handle designed to cook food on a stovetop.

skim   To remove fat or other material from the top of liquid.

steam   To suspend a food over boiling water and allow the heat of the steam to cook the food.

stew   To slowly cook pieces of food submerged in a liquid. Also a dish prepared using this method.

stir-fry   To cook small pieces of food in a wok or skillet over high heat, moving and turning the food quickly to cook all sides.

stock   A flavorful broth made by cooking meats and/or vegetables with seasonings until the liquid absorbs these flavors. The liquid is strained, and the solids are discarded. Stock can be eaten alone or used as a base for soups, stews, etc.

tapenade   A thick, chunky spread made from savory ingredients such as olives, lemon juice, and anchovies.

tarragon   A sweet, rich-smelling herb perfect with vegetables, seafood, chicken, and pork.

teriyaki   A Japanese-style sauce made of soy sauce, rice wine, ginger, and sugar.

thyme   A minty, zesty herb.

turmeric   A spicy, pungent yellow root. It's the source of the yellow color in many mustards.

tzatziki   A Greek dip traditionally made with Greek yogurt, cucumbers, garlic, and mint.

vinegar   An acidic liquid often made from fermented grapes, apples, or rice and used as a dressing and seasoning.

water chestnut   A white, crunchy, juicy tuber popular in many Asian dishes.

whisk   To rapidly mix, introducing air to the mixture.

white vinegar   Vinegar produced from grain.

whole grain   A grain derived from the seeds of grasses such as wheat, oats, rye, barley, buckwheat, corn, or rice.

whole-wheat flour   Wheat flour that contains the entire grain.

wild rice   A grass, often considered a rice, that has a rich, nutty flavor.

yeast   Tiny fungi that, when mixed with water, sugar, flour, and heat, release carbon dioxide bubbles that cause bread to rise.

zest   Small slivers of peel, usually from citrus fruit.

Index